Python: Embedded Systems for Beginners

By James Carlsen

Chapter 1: Introduction to Embedded Systems

What are Embedded Systems?

Embedded systems are dedicated computer systems designed for a specific purpose. They're often found within larger devices, working behind the scenes to make them function as intended. Here are some examples:

- **Smartphones**: The sensors, cameras, and displays in your phone don't work on their own; they're driven by embedded systems.
- **Cars**: Modern vehicles have dozens of embedded systems managing tasks like engine control, airbag deployment, and even infotainment systems.

Embedded systems differ from general-purpose computers (like desktops or laptops) in several ways:

1. **Single-Purpose**: They're designed to perform specific tasks and aren't intended for multitasking or running different software.
2. **Resource-Constrained**: Embedded systems often have limited processing power, memory, and other resources. This is why they're typically built around microcontrollers (like the ESP32 or STM32) rather than full-fledged processors.
3. **Real-Time Operation**: Many embedded systems must respond to external events promptly. They need to process inputs immediately to maintain synchrony with their environment.

Evolution of Embedded Programming

Embedded programming has evolved significantly over time. Early systems were programmed using low-level languages like assembly or C/C++, which offer fine-grained control but are difficult to work with due to their complexity and verbosity.

Over time, higher-level options have emerged that provide easier programming:

- **C++**: This is a superset of C with features like classes and templates that make it more expressive.

- **Embedded Domain-Specific Languages (DSLs)**: These are specialized languages designed for specific types of embedded systems. They abstract away many low-level details, making them easier to use.

Why Python in Embeded Development?

Python's simplicity, readability, and large developer community make it an attractive choice for embedded development:

1. **Quick Prototyping**: Python allows you to write code quickly, enabling faster prototyping compared to lower-level languages.
2. **Readability**: Python's syntax is clean and easy to understand, making your code more readable and maintainable.

Running Python on Embedded Systems

Python can run on embedded systems through specialized interpreters like:

- **MicroPython**: This is a lean implementation of Python designed for microcontrollers with limited resources.
- **CircuitPython**: Developed by Adafruit, CircuitPython is another Python interpreter for use in microcontroller boards like the BBC micro:bit and various Adafruit boards.

Benefits of Python for Embedded System Beginners

Using Python to learn embedded systems has several advantages:

- **Gentler Learning Curve**: Python's simplicity makes it easier to start with than lower-level languages.
- **Interactive Testing**: You can test your code directly in the Python interpreter, making debugging and experimentation easier.

However, there are trade-offs:

- **Performance**: High-level languages like Python typically have slower performance compared to low-level ones. They're often not used in performance-critical applications.

Real-World Examples of Python in Embedded Systems

Python's ease of use has led to its adoption in many embedded projects:

- **Simple IoT Sensors**: Python can be used to read sensor data (like temperature or humidity) and send it over the internet using protocols like MQTT.

```python
import machine
import utime


# Read DHT22 temperature and humidity sensor
dht = machine.DHT22(machine.Pin(4))
while True:
    dht.measure()
    temp = dht.temperature()
    hum = dht.humidity()
    print(f"Temperature: {temp:.1f}C, Humidity: {hum:.0f}%")
    utime.sleep(5)
```

- **Hobbyist Robots**: Python can be used to control robots like the BBC micro:bit robot. Here's a simple example of making an LED blink:

```python
import neopixel
import utime


# Initialize NeoPixel on pin 0 connected to an RGB LED.
np = neopixel.NeoPixel(machine.Pin(0), 1)


while True:
    for i in range(256):
```

```
np[0] = (i, 255 - i, abs(i - 128))
np.write()
utime.sleep_ms(10)
```

Chapter 2: Python Platforms for Embedded Systems

This chapter introduces you to three popular platforms that leverage the power of Python for embedded systems: MicroPython, CircuitPython, and Raspberry Pi. Each platform has its unique features and use cases, allowing you to choose the right tool for your project.

MicroPython

MicroPython is a lean implementation of Python 3 designed specifically for microcontrollers and embedded systems. It enables direct hardware control and bridges high-level coding with low-level embedded hardware. With MicroPython, you can write clean, readable code while still accessing the underlying hardware with ease.

Example: Blinking an LED on a PyBoard

Let's blink an LED using a PyBoard, which is a popular development board based on the STM32F4 microcontroller and supports MicroPython out of the box. First, connect your PyBoard to your computer via USB, then install the MicroPython firmware if you haven't already:

```python
# Connect to the board
from machine import Pin

led = Pin(13, Pin.OUT)  # Set GPIO pin 13 as output (LED connected to this pin)

while True:
    led.on()  # Turn on the LED
    time.sleep(0.5)  # Wait for half a second
    led.off()  # Turn off the LED
    time.sleep(0.5)  # Wait for another half-second before repeating
```

In this example, we use the Pin class from the machine module to control the LED connected to GPIO pin 13 on the PyBoard. The on() method turns the LED on, while off() turns it off. We use time.sleep() to introduce a delay between each state change.

CircuitPython

CircuitPython is Adafruit's beginner-friendly fork of MicroPython, designed with education in mind. It simplifies hardware programming by providing board-specific libraries and improving error messages compared to MicroPython. CircuitPython also adds support for more boards out of the box.

Example: Controlling NeoPixels on an Adafruit Feather M0 Express

Let's light up some NeoPixel LEDs using an Adafruit Feather M0 Express board running CircuitPython. First, make sure your board has the latest CircuitPython firmware installed. Then, connect your NeoPixel strip or individual pixels to the board's D1 pin.

```python
import time
from neopixel import NeoPixel

pixel_pin = 13  # Pin connected to NeoPixels (D1)
num_pixels = 8  # Number of NeoPixels connected
pixels = NeoPixel(pixel_pin, num_pixels)

while True:
    for i in range(num_pixels):
        pixels[i] = (0, 255, 0)  # Set pixel color to green
        pixels.show()  # Update the LED strip with new colors
        time.sleep(0.1)
```

In this example, we use the NeoPixel library to control a chain of NeoPixel LEDs connected to pin D1. We set each pixel's color one by one using RGB values and update the entire strip using pixels.show(). The time.sleep() function introduces a slight delay between each iteration.

Raspberry Pi

The Raspberry Pi is a single-board computer running full Python (CPython) on Linux, making it an excellent choice for more complex applications requiring operating system services. With its powerful processor and various available peripherals, the Raspberry Pi can handle tasks like camera processing and edge computing with ease.

Example: Controlling Motors with a Raspberry Pi Zero W

Let's control two DC motors using a Raspberry Pi Zero W, which has built-in wireless connectivity via Wi-Fi or Bluetooth. First, connect your motors to the RPi's GPIO pins using an L293D motor driver IC:

```python
import RPi.GPIO as GPIO
import time

# Motor control pins
motor1_a = 17
motor1_b = 18
motor2_a = 27
motor2_b = 22

GPIO.setmode(GPIO.BCM)
GPIO.setup([motor1_a, motor1_b, motor2_a, motor2_b], GPIO.OUT)

def forward(motor):
    GPIO.output(motor[0], GPIO.HIGH)
    GPIO.output(motor[1], GPIO.LOW)

def backward(motor):
    GPIO.output(motor[0], GPIO.LOW)
    GPIO.output(motor[1], GPIO.HIGH)
```

```
def stop(motor):
    GPIO.output(motor[0], GPIO.LOW)
    GPIO.output(motor[1], GPIO.LOW)

while True:
    forward([motor1_a, motor1_b])
    time.sleep(1)
    backward([motor2_a, motor2_b])
    time.sleep(1)
    stop([motor1_a, motor1_b])
    stop([motor2_a, motor2_b])
    time.sleep(2)
```

In this example, we use the RPi.GPIO library to control two DC motors connected through an L293D driver IC. We define functions for forward, backward, and stopping each motor. In the main loop, we alternate between moving each motor forward and backward with a brief pause in between.

Choosing the Right Tool

When selecting between MicroPython, CircuitPython, or Raspberry Pi, consider your project's requirements:

1. **MicroPython/CircuitPython**:
   - Ideal for resource-limited microcontrollers.
   - Best suited for low-power applications, simple tasks, and small-scale projects with direct hardware control.

2. **Raspberry Pi**:
   - Great for more complex applications requiring an operating system.
   - Perfect for edge computing, camera processing, and other tasks that demand greater processing power and OS services.

Popular Boards

Here's a list of popular boards compatible with MicroPython/CircuitPython or Raspberry Pi:

- **MicroPython/CircuitPython**:
    - PyBoard
    - ESP32 (e.g., WROVER, DOIT)
    - Adafruit Feather (e.g., ESP8266, ESP32)
    - Circuit Playground Express
- **Raspberry Pi**:
    - Raspberry Pi Pico
    - Raspberry Pi Zero (W, WH)
    - Raspberry Pi 4 Model B
    - Raspberry Pi 3 Model B+

In conclusion, Python platforms like MicroPython, CircuitPython, and Raspberry Pi offer powerful tools for embedded systems development. Choose the right platform based on your project's requirements to make the most of Python's simplicity and efficiency in your embedded projects.

Chapter 3: Setting Up Your MicroPython and CircuitPython Environment

Selecting a Microcontroller Board

MicroPython and CircuitPython support various microcontroller boards. Here are some popular options:

- **ESP32**: A low-cost, Wi-Fi enabled board with dual-core processor. It's great for IoT projects.
    - *Specs*: Dual-core 240 MHz Xtensa LX6 microprocessor, 512 KB SRAM, 4 MB PSRAM (optional), Wi-Fi and Bluetooth connectivity.
- **BBC micro:bit**: A small, single-board computer designed for kids to learn coding. It has built-in sensors and displays.
    - *Specs*: Nordic nRF51822 ARM Cortex-M0 processor running at 16 MHz, 256 KB Flash, 16 KB SRAM, accelerometer, magnetometer, light sensor, and a display consisting of 25 LEDs.
- **Raspberry Pi Pico**: A low-cost, high-performance microcontroller board based on the RP2040 chip.
    - *Specs*: Dual-core Arm Cortex-M0+ processor running at 133 MHz, 264 KB SRAM, 2 MB on-board Flash memory.
- **Adafruit Circuit Playground Express**: A versatile board designed for education and DIY projects. It has built-in sensors and NeoPixels.
    - *Specs*: ATmega32u4 microcontroller running at 8 MHz, 32 KB Flash, 2.5 KB SRAM, light sensor, temperature sensor, joystick, speaker, and eight NeoPixel LEDs.

Installing MicroPython Firmware

ESP32 using esptool.py

1. First, install the esptool.py tool if you haven't already:

```
pip install esptool.py
```

2. Download the latest MicroPython firmware for ESP32 from the official website (https://micropython.org/download/esp32/).

3. Use esptool.py to flash the firmware to your ESP32 board:

```
esptool.py --port /dev/ttyUSB0 write_flash --flash_size=detect 0 micropython.bin
```

Replace /dev/ttyUSB0 with the appropriate COM port for your board.

RP2040 using UF2 files

1. Download the latest MicroPython firmware for RP2040 from the official website (https://micropython.org/download/rp2/).

2. Drag and drop the downloaded .uf2 file onto your Raspberry Pi Pico's bootloader mode:

    –   Hold down the BOOT button while plugging in the Pico.
    –   Wait until the Pico appears as a USB mass storage device, then release the BOOT button.
    –   Drag and drop the .uf2 file onto the Pico's drive.

Getting Started with CircuitPython

CircuitPython boards like Adafruit's come pre-flashed with CircuitPython firmware. You can start using them immediately for simple projects. For other boards, you can install CircuitPython via drag-and-drop:

1. Download the latest CircuitPython UF2 file from the official website (https://circuitpython.org/board).

2. Follow the same process as installing MicroPython on RP2040 to flash your board with CircuitPython.

Connecting to REPL

To connect to the Read-Evaluate-Print Loop (REPL) over USB serial for live Python commands:

1. Open a terminal/command prompt.
2. Find your device's COM port (e.g., /dev/ttyUSB0 on Linux, COM3 on Windows).
3. Connect using a terminal emulator like screen, minicom, or PuTTY:
   - On Linux/MacOS:

     screen /dev/ttyUSB0 115200 --raw

   - On Windows (using PuTTY):
     - Set Serial to your COM port.
     - Set Speed to 115200 baud.
     - Connect.

You should now be connected to the REPL, and you can type Python commands directly.

Using IDEs

Thonny

Thonny is a simple Python IDE with built-in support for MicroPython. Here's how to use it:

1. Install Thonny from its official website (https://thonny.org/).
2. Open Thonny and go to Tools > Options.
3. Under the "Microcontroller" tab, select your board and interface.
4. Click OK.
5. Now you can write Python code in Thonny and upload it to your board using the green arrow icon.

Mu

Mu is another simple IDE designed for learning programming with microcontrollers:

1. Install Mu from its official website (https://mu-editor.com/).
2. Connect your board via USB.
3. Open Mu, then go to File > Select Board.
4. Choose your board and click OK.
5. Now you can write Python code in Mu and upload it to your board using the green arrow icon.

Managing Device Filesystem

MicroPython Flash vs CircuitPython's CIRCUITPY USB Drive

MicroPython stores its filesystem in flash memory on the microcontroller, while CircuitPython uses a virtual filesystem on a USB drive named CIRCUITPY.

To access files on your board:

- **MicroPython**: You can use the built-in os module to list files and directories, e.g., os.listdir().
- **CircuitPython**: Remove the board from the USB port, then reinsert it. The CIRCUITPY drive will appear containing your project's code and data.

Running a "Hello, world" Test or Blinking LED

Here's a simple "Hello, world" program in MicroPython:

```
print("Hello, world!")
```

And here's how to blink an LED using the built-in machine module on a board like ESP32:

```
import machine
import utime
```

```
led = machine.Pin(2, machine.Pin.OUT)

while True:
    led.on()
    utime.sleep(0.5)
    led.off()
    utime.sleep(0.5)
```

Troubleshooting Connection Issues

If you're having trouble connecting to your board:

1. **Check drivers**: Ensure your board has the correct drivers installed on your computer.

2. **Find the right COM port**: Use tools like lsusb (Linux/MacOS) or Device Manager (Windows) to find the correct COM port for your board.

3. **Enter bootloader mode**: Some boards, like the ESP32, need to be put into bootloader mode before flashing new firmware. Refer to your board's documentation for instructions on entering bootloader mode.

Chapter 4: Setting Up the Raspberry Pi for Python-Based Embedded Projects

Welcome to Chapter 4! In this chapter, we'll set up your Raspberry Pi (RPi) for Python-based embedded projects. We'll cover everything from flashing the operating system onto an SD card and booting the board to installing hardware control libraries and verifying your setup by blinking an LED.

Flashing Raspberry Pi OS onto an SD card

Before you start, make sure you have:

- A fresh microSD card (at least 8GB)
- A computer running Windows, macOS, or Linux
- The latest version of **Raspberry Pi Imager** for your operating system: https://www.raspberrypi.com/software/

Here's how to flash Raspberry Pi OS onto your SD card:

1. Insert the microSD card into your computer's card reader.
2. Open Raspberry Pi Imager and select Raspberry Pi OS from the dropdown menu.
3. Choose the appropriate version for your RPi model (e.g., Lite for minimal desktop environment).
4. Click on the **SELECT STORAGE** button, then choose your microSD card from the list.
5. Click the **WRITE** button to flash Raspberry Pi OS onto your SD card.

Once completed, safely eject the microSD card and insert it into your RPi.

Booting the Raspberry Pi board

Connect your RPi's essential components:

- MicroUSB power supply

- HDMI cable to a monitor (if using keyboard/monitor)
- Ethernet cable or Wi-Fi for internet access
- A USB keyboard and mouse (if using keyboard/monitor)

Power up your RPi. After about 30 seconds, you should see the Raspberry Pi logo on your screen if using a monitor, or you can SSH into it using ssh pi@<your_rpi_ip>.

Enabling GPIO, I²C, SPI via raspi-config

To enable GPIO, I²C, and SPI for hardware interfacing:

1. Connect to your RPi via SSH: ssh pi@<your_rpi_ip>.
2. Once connected, type sudo raspi-config to open the configuration tool.
3. Select Interfacing Options.
4. Enable **GPIO** by selecting Yes.
5. Enable **I²C** and **SPI** using the same steps.
6. Exit the configuration tool and reboot your RPi.

Accessing the Pi via keyboard/monitor or SSH for headless operation

To use SSH for headless operation:

1. Edit the /home/pi/.bashrc file with nano ~/.bashrc.

2. Add your preferred Wi-Fi credentials to the end of the file:

   printf "country=AU\nctrl_interface=/run/wpa_supplicant\nupdate_config=1\n" >
   /etc/wpa_country.conf
   wpa_passphrase <your_SSID> <your_password> >>
   /etc/wpa_supplicant/wpa_supplicant.conf

Save and close the file, then reboot your RPi. After rebooting, you can SSH into it using ssh pi@<your_rpi_ip>.

Installing/updating Python 3 and choosing an editor/IDE (Thonny)

Python 3 is pre-installed on Raspberry Pi OS. To update it:

```
sudo apt update
sudo apt upgrade python3
```

For Thonny, a simple IDE for beginners:

1. Open the terminal.
2. Type sudo apt install thonny and press Enter.
3. Press Y to confirm installation, then Enter to continue.

Once installed, launch Thonny from your applications menu or by typing thonny in the terminal.

Installing hardware-control libraries (RPi.GPIO, gpiozero)

For RPi.GPIO:

```
sudo apt install RPi.GPIO python3-rpi.gpio
```

For gpiozero:

```
pip3 install gpiozero
```

Verify your installations with:

```
import RPi.GPIO as GPIO
from gpiozero import LED

print(GPIO.VERSION)
led = LED(17)  # Check if the LED object is created successfully
```

Verifying setup by blinking an LED via gpiozero

Connect an LED to pin 17 (GPIO 17) and ground:

```
from gpiozero import LED, LEDBoard
import time

led_board = LEDBoard(17)
while True:
    led_board.on()
    time.sleep(0.5)
    led_board.off()
    time.sleep(0.5)
```

Press Ctrl+C to stop the script.

Understanding Linux vs. bare-metal timing/reliability

- **Linux**: Uses a scheduler for multitasking, leading to less predictable timings but more reliability.
- **Bare-Metal**: Has precise timing control but lacks reliability and must manage resources manually.

Electrical considerations: 3.3 V logic, current limits, resistors, level shifting

- RPi works with **3.3V logic**, not 5V!
- Current limit for each GPIO pin is **16mA**.
- Use **resistors** to limit current and protect your components.
- For interfacing with 5V devices, use a **level shifter** or voltage dividers.

Chapter 5: Python Programming Essentials for Embedded Systems

This chapter serves as a refresher on essential Python programming concepts tailored to embedded systems development using MicroPython and CircuitPython. We'll focus on clear, concise examples relevant to embedded systems.

Python Syntax Refresher

Variables and Data Types

In Python, variables store data values. Here are some basic data types:

```python
# Integer
num = 10


# Float
decimal = 3.14


# String
message = "Hello, World!"


# Boolean
is_true = True
```

Sensor Context

Embedded systems often interact with sensors. Let's consider a simple temperature sensor:

```python
import sensor


temp_celsius = sensor.read_temp()  # Read temperature in Celsius
temp_fahrenheit = temp_celsius * 9/5 + 32  # Convert to Fahrenheit
```

Control Structures: if/else and Loops for Polling/Blinking

Conditional Statements (if/elif/else)

```python
# Example: Turn on LED if temperature is above threshold
if temp_celsius > 25:
    led.on()
elif temp_celsius < 10:
    print("Temperature is too low!")
else:
    led.off()
```

Loops for Polling and Blinking

While Loop (for polling)

```python
# Example: Monitor button press until released
button_pressed = False
while not button_pressed:
    if button.is_pressed():
        button_pressed = True
```

For Loop with range() (for blinking)

```python
# Example: Blink LED every second for 5 times
for _ in range(5):
    led.on()
    time.sleep(1)
    led.off()
    time.sleep(1)
```

Organizing Code with Functions/Modules

Defining and Using Functions

```python
# Define function to convert Celsius to Fahrenheit
def celsius_to_fahrenheit(celsius):
    return celsius * 9/5 + 32
```

```
# Use the function
temp_f = celsius_to_fahrenheit(temp_celsius)
```

Importing Modules

```
import sensor
import time
import board


# Now you can use the functions and constants from these modules
```

Using the REPL for Quick Testing

The Read-Eval-Print Loop (REPL) is great for quick testing. You can interact with your code line by line:

```
>>> temp_celsius = 25
>>> if temp_celsius > 25:
...     led.on()
...
led.on()
```

Timing with time.sleep() and Non-Blocking Loops

Blocking Delay (time.sleep())

```
# Example: Delay for 1 second
time.sleep(1)
```

Non-Blocking Loop with *asyncio*

For tasks that should continue running while waiting for other events, use asyncio:

```
import asyncio


async def wait_for_button():
```

```
while not button.is_pressed():
    await asyncio.sleep(0.1)  # Don't block the main loop
```

Debugging with print() and try/except

print()

```
# Example: Print temperature readings for debugging
print(f"Temperature in Celsius: {temp_celsius}")
print(f"Temperature in Fahrenheit: {temp_f}")
```

try/except

Handle exceptions to prevent your program from crashing:

```
try:
    reading = sensor.read_temp()
except OSError as e:
    print(f"Error reading temperature: {e}")
```

MicroPython/CircuitPython Core Features vs. Limitations

MicroPython and CircuitPython offer many core features but have some limitations due to their resource-constrained nature.

Core Features: - Real-time performance - Built-in hardware support (I2C, SPI, ADC, etc.) - AsyncIO for non-blocking I/O - Microcontroller-specific libraries (e.g., neopixel)

Limitations: - Limited memory resources (GC.collect() to manage) - Some advanced Python features may not be supported or behave differently

Writing Memory-Efficient Python

To minimize garbage collection and optimize embedded system performance:

- Avoid large data structures
- Reduce object creation
- Use built-in types where possible (e.g., bytearray instead of bytes)
```
```

- Enable aggressive garbage collection (gc.enable())

Example: Use bytearray for efficient string manipulation.

```
msg = bytearray(b"Hello, World!")
msg[7:] = b"\x00\x00\x00"
print(msg.decode())  # Prints: Hello,
```

Chapter 6: Understanding Microcontroller Hardware Basics

This chapter will introduce you to the fundamental components and concepts behind microcontrollers (MCUs), with a focus on those that work well with Python. We'll explore their anatomy, compare them to microprocessors, and learn how to read datasheets and pinouts. Finally, we'll delve into MicroPython's runtime and constraints.

Microcontroller Anatomy

A microcontroller is essentially a System on Chip (SoC) containing several key components:

1. **CPU Core**: The brain of the MCU where instructions are executed. Most MCUs used in embedded systems employ ARM Cortex-M series cores, which are known for their efficiency and low power consumption.

2. **Clock**: Generates the timing signals that synchronize the operation of all other components. It can be an internal oscillator or driven by an external clock source.

3. **Flash Memory**: Stores the firmware (program) to be executed by the CPU core. It retains data even when powered off, thanks to its non-volatile nature.

4. **RAM (Random Access Memory)**: Temporary storage for data and instructions used during program execution. Unlike flash memory, RAM is volatile and loses its contents upon power loss.

5. **Peripherals**:

   - **General Purpose Input/Output (GPIO)**: Pins that can be configured as inputs or outputs to interact with external hardware.
   - **Analog-to-Digital Converter (ADC)**: Convert analog signals (voltage) into digital data for the MCU to process.

- **Digital-to-Analog Converter (DAC)**: Converts digital data from the MCU back into analog signals.
- **Timers/Counters**: Generate timing signals or measure time intervals. They can also generate interrupts upon specific events.
- **Communication Interfaces** (e.g., UART, SPI, I2C): Enable communication with other devices and peripherals.

Here's a simple example of accessing GPIO pins using MicroPython on an ESP32:

```python
from machine import Pin

led = Pin(2, Pin.OUT)  # Set GPIO2 as output for an LED

while True:
    led.value(1)  # Turn on the LED
    sleep(0.5)
    led.value(0)  # Turn off the LED
    sleep(0.5)
```

Firmware Execution Model

MicroPython runs Python bytecode interpretively on microcontrollers, enabling you to write high-level code while still having fine-grained control over hardware.

MCU vs. Microprocessor

The main difference lies in their intended use and what's included on the chip:

- MCUs are designed for embedded systems, with integrated peripherals like GPIO, ADC, timers, etc., and often don't run an operating system (though they can).
- Microprocessors are general-purpose CPUs without built-in peripherals. They typically run under an OS to manage system resources.

Reading Datasheets and Pinouts

Datasheets provide crucial information about your MCU, including:

- **Voltages and Currents**: Operating voltages, supply current, pin current drive capability, etc.
- **Special-function Pins**: Pins with additional capabilities beyond GPIO (e.g., dedicated clock input pins).

Pinouts show the physical arrangement of pins on the MCU package. They help in designing PCBs or selecting appropriate adapters/boards.

Common MCU Families

Cortex-M Series

ARM's Cortex-M series (e.g., M0, M3, M4, M7) are popular in embedded systems due to their low power consumption and efficiency. They are used in many MCUs like STM32, Nordic nRF5x, etc.

ESP32

A popular choice for IoT applications, the ESP32 is a low-cost, low-power system on a chip with integrated Wi-Fi and dual-mode Bluetooth. It features a Tensilica Xtensa LX6 microprocessor, along with various peripherals like ADC, DAC, I2C, SPI, UART, etc.

MicroPython Runtime

MicroPython's runtime includes:

- **Bootloader**: Initializes the MCU, loads the firmware from flash memory into RAM, and starts executing it.
- **Flash/RAM Usage**: MicroPython uses a part of the flash memory for storing its own code and data structures. It uses RAM for running your scripts and storing variables.

Clock and timing implications are important to consider:

- **CPU Clock Speed**: Higher speeds mean more instructions can be executed per second, but they also consume more power.
- **System Clock**: Drives peripheral devices like UART, I2C, SPI, etc. It often runs at a lower frequency than the CPU clock for better power efficiency.

Constraints: Limited RAM/CPU Speed

Microcontrollers have limited resources compared to full-fledged computers or single-board computers (SBCs) like the Raspberry Pi:

- **RAM**: Typically in the range of kilobytes, which limits the size and complexity of tasks that can be performed.
- **CPU Speed**: Relatively slower than desktop processors, impacting performance when executing complex computations.

Example: Avoiding heavy computational tasks on an ESP32

```python
# Bad practice: heavy computation in a loop drains resources quickly
while True:
    sum(range(10000))  # Computes the sum of numbers from 0 to 9999
```

Instead, offload heavy computations to more powerful devices when possible or optimize your code to minimize resource usage.

Chapter 7: Electronics Fundamentals and Breadboard Prototyping

Understanding the Basics

Embedded systems interact with the physical world through electronics. This chapter introduces you to fundamental electronic concepts and helps you prototype your designs on a breadboard.

Voltage, Current, Resistance, and Ohm's Law

- **Voltage (V)** is like pressure in an electrical circuit. It drives current flow.
- **Current (I)** is the rate of flow of electric charge, measured in Amperes (A).
- **Resistance (R)** opposes the flow of current.

Ohm's law states that voltage (V), current (I), and resistance (R) are related by the equation:

$$V = IR$$

Example: A 1 kilo-Ohm (kΩ) resistor connected to a 3.3V power supply will have a current flowing through it calculated as follows:

$$I = V / R = 3.3V / 1kΩ = 0.0033A \text{ or } 3.3mA$$

Power Considerations

- **3.3V vs. 5V Logic**: Most microcontrollers have a logic voltage of either 3.3V or 5V. Connecting them incorrectly can damage your components.
- **Common Ground (GND)**: All your components should share a common ground to avoid unexpected behavior.

Breadboard Prototyping

Breadboard Layout and Power Rails

A breadboard has power rails on the sides where you connect power supply pins of your components, and signal rows in the middle for connecting component legs.

Jumper Techniques

Jumper wires are used to connect component legs together. To avoid shorts, always ensure your connections are clean and neat.

Example: Connecting an LED's positive leg (anode) to 3.3V power rail and its negative leg (cathode) to GND makes the LED glow.

```
LED+
| |
+---3.3V
|
GND
```

Basic Components

LEDs (Light Emitting Diodes)

LEDs have a positive leg (anode, longer) and a negative leg (cathode, shorter). Always connect them with a resistor in series to prevent excess current.

Example: Connecting an LED as shown above with a 330Ω resistor in series.

```
LED+-------330Ω------3.3V
   |
GND
```

Resistors

Resistors have color bands indicating their resistance value and tolerance. The gold or silver band is the multiplier, and each band before it represents one digit.

Example: A brown-black-red (BBR) resistor has a value of 100Ω (±5%).

Buttons/Switches

Buttons are normally open (NO), so they pull their connected pin to high logic level when pressed. Use pull-down resistors to avoid floating inputs.

Example: Connecting a momentary button with a 10kΩ pull-down resistor:

GND---10kΩ------Button---|---Pin

Sensors

Sensors like photoresistors and temperature sensors have analog outputs. They require additional circuitry (voltage divider, signal conditioning) for interfacing with microcontrollers.

Reading Schematics to Breadboard Mapping

Schematics represent electrical circuits using symbols connected by lines. Understanding schematics helps you translate designs onto breadboards accurately.

Building an LED Circuit with Resistor

Let's build the LED circuit shown in the schematic above:

1. Connect one leg of a 330Ω resistor to the power rail (3.3V) and the other leg to the LED's positive leg.
2. Connect the LED's negative leg to GND.
3. Test your circuit using a multimeter set to continuity test mode.

Multimeter Basics

A multimeter is an essential tool for troubleshooting and verifying electrical circuits.

- **Voltage (V)**: Measures voltage difference between two points.

   $V = IR$

- **Continuity (Beep)**: Tests if there's a complete circuit between two points. It beeps when resistance is low (<50Ω).

Example: Measure the voltage across the LED in our previous example:

```
3.3V---LED+-------330Ω------Multimeter
   |
GND
```

Pull-up/Pull-down Resistors

Pull-up/pull-down resistors help avoid floating inputs by pulling pins to a known logic level when no external signal is present.

- **Pull-up**: Connect resistor (10kΩ - 47kΩ) between pin and VCC/3.3V.
- **Pull-down**: Connect resistor (10kΩ - 47kΩ) between pin and GND.

Example: Using a 10kΩ pull-down resistor with a button:

```
GND---10kΩ------Button---|---Pin
```

This way, the pin reads LOW when the button is not pressed and HIGH when it's pressed.

Chapter 8: Digital Output - Blinking LEDs and GPIO Basics

In this chapter, we'll explore digital output using Python on embedded systems like microcontrollers (MCUs) and the Raspberry Pi. We'll focus on controlling General Purpose Input/Output (GPIO) pins to blink LEDs and understand the basics of GPIO operations.

GPIO Pins for Digital Output (HIGH/LOW)

MCUs and Pis have GPIO pins that can be configured as digital inputs or outputs. For digital output, we're interested in setting a pin's state to HIGH (logic 1) or LOW (logic 0). To control LEDs, we'll set the pin to HIGH to turn it on and LOW to turn it off.

Configuring Output Pins in Code

To configure a GPIO pin as an output, we need to use appropriate libraries:

On Microcontrollers (like ESP32/ESP8266)

Using machine.Pin:

```python
from machine import Pin


led = Pin(2, Pin.OUT)  # Set pin 2 as OUTPUT
```

On Raspberry Pi (using RPi.GPIO library)

First, install the library using:

```
sudo apt-get update
sudo apt-get install python-rpi.gpio python3-rpi.gpio
```

Then in your Python script:

```python
import RPi.GPIO as GPIO
```

```
GPIO.setmode(GPIO.BCM)
led = 18  # Set pin 18 (GPIO pin number) as output
GPIO.setup(led, GPIO.OUT)
```

Using digitalio on both platforms

If you're using the adafruit-circuitpython library, which supports both MCUs and Pis, use DigitalInOut:

```
import board
import digitalio

led = digitalio.DigitalInOut(board.LED)  # Set LED pin as OUTPUT
led.direction = digitalio.Direction.OUTPUT
```

Wiring LEDs with Series Resistors

To protect your LED from excessive current, wire it in series with a resistor:

Calculate the resistor value using Ohm's law: $R = (V\_supply - V\_LED) / I\_LED$, where I_LED is the current your LED can handle safely (usually 20-30mA).

Blink Program: HIGH/delay/LOW Loop

Now let's blink an LED using a simple HIGH/Low loop with delay:

On Microcontrollers:
```
from machine import Pin
import utime

led = Pin(2, Pin.OUT)

while True:
    led.on()  # Set pin to HIGH (turn LED on)
    utime.sleep(0.5)  # Delay for half a second
```

```
led.off()  # Set pin to LOW (turn LED off)
utime.sleep(0.5)  # Delay again
```

On Raspberry Pi:

```
import RPi.GPIO as GPIO
import time

led = 18
GPIO.setmode(GPIO.BCM)
GPIO.setup(led, GPIO.OUT)

while True:
    GPIO.output(led, GPIO.HIGH)  # Set pin to HIGH (turn LED on)
    time.sleep(0.5)  # Delay for half a second
    GPIO.output(led, GPIO.LOW)  # Set pin to LOW (turn LED off)
    time.sleep(0.5)  # Delay again
```

Adjusting Delay for Blink Rate

To change the blink rate, adjust the delay value:

```
while True:
    led.on()
    utime.sleep(1)  # Increase delay to 1 second
    led.off()
    utime.sleep(1)
```

Continuous Operation via while True

The above examples run indefinitely. To stop them, press Ctrl+C in the terminal or use a hardware reset.

Beyond LEDs: Buzzers, Relays, and Motors

You can control other devices like buzzers (by pulsing pins quickly), relays (using transistors or MOSFETs), and motors (using driver circuits) using similar techniques:

```
buzzer = Pin(5, Pin.OUT)
while True:
    buzzer.on()
    utime.sleep(0.1)
    buzzer.off()
    utime.sleep(0.1)
```

Best Practices: Cleanup and Safe Current

Always clean up GPIO resources when done:

On Microcontrollers:

```
led.deinit()  # Free up resources
```

On Raspberry Pi:

```
GPIO.cleanup()  # Reset GPIO to inputs with no pull-up/down
```

Ensure your devices operate within safe current limits (10-20mA max for LEDs). Using resistors and calculating current using Ohm's law helps protect components from damage.

Chapter 9: Digital Input - Reading Buttons and Switches

In this chapter, we'll explore how to read digital inputs from buttons and switches using Python in an embedded systems context. We'll cover configuring GPIO pins as inputs, understanding pull-up/pull-down resistors, reading button states, debouncing strategies, and using interrupts for responsive input.

Configuring GPIO as Input

To configure a GPIO pin as an input, we use the Pin.IN mode when initializing the pin. Here's how you can do it:

```python
from machine import Pin

# Configure GPIO16 as input
button = Pin(16, Pin.IN)
```

Alternatively, you can use the DigitalInOut class or GPIO.setup() function to achieve the same result:

```python
from digitalio import DigitalInOut, Direction
import board

# Using DigitalInOut
button = DigitalInOut(board.GPIO16)
button.direction = Direction.INPUT

# Using GPIO.setup()
import GPIO
GP.IO.setup(16, GP.IO.IN)
```

Wiring Buttons with Pull-up/Pull-down Resistors

When using buttons or switches as inputs, it's essential to consider the resistor network. By default, buttons are open-circuit when not pressed and create a closed circuit when pressed. To avoid floating values, we use pull-up or pull-down resistors.

- **Pull-up**: The button pulls the voltage down from 3V3 (or VCC) when pressed.
- **Pull-down**: The button pulls the voltage up to ground (GND) when pressed.

Here's how you can configure each:

```python
from machine import Pin


# Pull-up resistor using Pin.PULL_UP
button_up = Pin(16, Pin.IN, pull=Pin.PULL_UP)


# Pull-down resistor using external resistor connected between button and GND
button_down = Pin(17, Pin.IN)
```

Enabling Internal Pulls (Pin.PULL_UP)

Some platforms support internal pulls. To enable an internal pull-up resistor:

```python
from machine import Pin


button_int_pull_up = Pin(16, Pin.IN, pull=Pin.PULL_UP)
```

Reading Pin Value for Button State

To read the button state (pressed or not), we use pin.value(). By default, value() returns 0 (False) when the pin is grounded and 1 (True) when it's open-circuit.

```python
while True:
    if button.value() == 0:  # Button is pressed
        print("Button pressed!")
```

Debouncing Strategies

Buttons have a mechanical bounce effect that can cause multiple readings of the same state. To avoid this, we use debouncing strategies like delays or state machines.

Delay: Wait for some time after detecting a button press before reading its state again.

```python
import utime


while True:
    if button.value() == 0:  # Button is pressed
        print("Button pressed!")
        while button.value() == 0: pass  # Wait for button release
        utime.sleep(0.2)  # Debounce delay to avoid bouncing effects
```

State Machine: Track the button's state and only change it when a transition is detected.

```python
button_state = False


while True:
    current_state = button.value()
    if current_state != button_state:  # State transition detected
        print(f"Button {'pressed' if current_state else 'released'}!")
        button_state = current_state
```

Interrupts/Callbacks with pin.irq() for Responsive Input

To react instantly to button presses, we can use interrupts and callbacks.

```python
from machine import Pin


def button_irq.handler(pin):
    print("Button pressed!")
```

```
button = Pin(16, Pin.IN)
button.irq(trigger=Pin.IRQ_RISING | Pin.IRQ_FALLING, handler=button_irq)  # React to
both presses and releases
```

Example: Toggle LED on Button Press

Let's combine some of the concepts above to toggle an LED when a button is pressed.

```python
from machine import Pin

led = Pin(25, Pin.OUT)
button = Pin(16, Pin.IN, pull=Pin.PULL_UP)

while True:
    if not button.value():  # Button is pressed (active-low configuration)
        led.toggle()
        while not button.value(): pass  # Debounce using delay
```

Ensuring Stable Input Sensing and Switch Quality

To ensure stable input sensing:

- Use appropriate resistor networks for your buttons/switches.
- Consider the debouncing strategy suitable for your application.
- Choose appropriate GPIO pins with sufficient voltage/tolerance levels.
- Shield your circuits from noise when possible.

Chapter 10: Timers and PWM – Generating Signals and Controlling Brightness

In this chapter, we'll explore how to generate precise signals and control brightness using timers and Pulse Width Modulation (PWM) with Python on embedded systems. We'll start by understanding hardware timers for precise events and then dive into the concept of PWM for analog-like output.

Hardware Timers for Precise Events

Hardware timers are special-purpose registers used to generate periodic interrupts at a specific interval. They are essential for creating precise timing in your embedded system. In Python, you can use the machine module's Timer class on microcontrollers like the ESP32 to create hardware timers.

Here's a simple example of how to create a timer that triggers an interrupt every second:

```python
import machine

def timer_callback(timer):
    print("One second has passed!")

timer = machine.Timer(-1)
timer.init(period=1000, mode=machine.Timer.PERIODIC, callback=timer_callback)
```

In this example, the Timer is initialized with a period of 1000 milliseconds (1 second), and it will call the timer_callback function every second.

Introduction to PWM: Duty Cycle Concept for Analog-Like Output

Pulse Width Modulation (PWM) is a technique used to control voltage or current by rapidly turning a device on and off. The duty cycle is the ratio of the pulse duration to the period, expressed as a percentage. It determines the average value of the signal, providing an analog-like output from digital systems.

For instance, if you have a PWM signal with a frequency (f) of 1 kHz and a duty cycle (d) of 50%, the voltage will be at its peak for half of each second (500 ms), creating an average voltage that's half of the peak voltage:

Average Voltage = Peak Voltage * Duty Cycle
Average Voltage = V_peak * (d / 100)

Configuring PWM in Python

Python provides several libraries to configure and control PWM on embedded systems. We'll explore machine.PWM, pwmio.PWMOut, and gpiozero.PWMLED using simple examples.

machine.PWM

The machine.PWM class can be used to create a PWM signal on GPIO pins:

```python
import machine


pwm = machine.PWM(machine.Pin(2), freq=500, duty_u16=32768)  # Create a 50% duty cycle PWM signal at 500 Hz on GPIO2
```

pwmio.PWMOut

The pwmio.PWMOut class offers more control over the PWM signal:

```python
import pwmio


pwm = pwmio.PWMOut(Pin(2), freq=500, duty_cycle=0.5)  # Create a 50% duty cycle PWM signal at 500 Hz on GPIO2
```

gpiozero.PWMLED

gpiozero.PWMLED is a convenient class for controlling LEDs with PWM:

```
from gpiozero import PWMLED

led = PWMLED(2)  # Create a PWM LED object connected to GPIO2
led.value = 0.5  # Set the LED brightness to half (50% duty cycle)
```

Fading an LED via Duty Cycle Sweep

To fade an LED in and out, you can sweep the duty cycle from 0% to 100% over time:

```
from gpiozero import PWMLED
import time

led = PWMLED(2)

for dc in range(0, 65535, 100):  # Sweep from 0% to 100% duty cycle (65535 is max
value for u16)
    led.duty_cycle = dc / 65535
    time.sleep(0.01)  # Wait for 10 ms before changing duty cycle
```

Servo Control: 50 Hz PWM for Angle Setting

Servo motors use PWM signals to control their position. A typical servo expects a PWM signal with a frequency of 50 Hz, where the pulse duration determines the motor's angle:

```
from gpiozero import PWMLED
import time

led = PWMLED(2)  # Servo connected to GPIO2

def set_angle(angle):
    dc = (angle / 180.0 + 0.5) * 65535
    led.duty_cycle = dc / 65535
```

```
set_angle(90)  # Set servo to middle position (90 degrees)
time.sleep(1)
set_angle(180)  # Set servo to maximum clockwise position
```

Motor Speed Control with PWM via Driver/Transistor

To control motor speed using PWM, you'll need a driver or transistor circuit to handle the current. Here's an example using a MOSFET and the pwmio.PWMOut class:

```python
import pwmio

motor = pwmio.PWMOut(Pin(2), freq=100)  # Motor connected to GPIO2 through a
MOSFET

def set_speed(speed):
    motor.duty_cycle = speed / 100.0

set_speed(50)  # Set motor speed to half (50%)
```

PWM Frequency Considerations: Flicker and Motor Smoothness

Choosing the right PWM frequency is crucial for avoiding flicker in LEDs and ensuring smooth operation of motors:

- For LED dimming, frequencies above 20 kHz are usually sufficient to avoid visible flickering.
- For servo control, a frequency of around 50 Hz is typically used.
- For motor speed control, higher frequencies (e.g., 15-20 kHz) can result in smoother operation.

Using Timers or Loops for Periodic Tasks

To perform periodic tasks like generating PWM signals or measuring time intervals, you can use hardware timers or loops with time.sleep():

```python
import machine
import time


# Using a hardware timer to trigger an interrupt every 10 ms
timer = machine.Timer(-1)
counter = 0


def callback(timer):
    global counter
    print(f"Counter: {counter}")
    counter += 1


timer.init(period=10, mode=machine.Timer.PERIODIC, callback=callback)

# Using a loop to sleep for 10 ms every iteration
while True:
    time.sleep_ms(10)
    print("Hello from loop!")
```

Chapter 11: Analog Input - Reading Sensors with ADC

In the digital world of embedded systems, sensors often produce analog signals. These signals must be converted into digital form using an Analog-to-Digital Converter (ADC) before they can be processed by a microcontroller. In this chapter, we'll explore how to read these analog signals using Python on popular microcontrollers like the BBC micro:bit and the CircuitPython boards.

Understanding Analog vs Digital Signals

Analog signals are continuous, varying smoothly over time. They represent real-world quantities like temperature, light intensity, or voltage. On the other hand, digital signals are discrete, representing only two states: high (1) or low (0).

Since microcontrollers operate on digital signals, we need an ADC to convert analog signals into digital form for processing.

Configuring ADC Pins

Microcontrollers with built-in ADCs allow direct reading of analog signals. In Python, we use the machine.ADC module for MicroPython and analogio.AnalogIn for CircuitPython to configure ADC pins.

```
# MicroPython (BBC micro:bit)
import machine
adc = machine.ADC(26)  # Pin P0 on BBC micro:bit is connected to an analog sensor

# CircuitPython (Trinket M0 or Gemma M0)
import analogio
adc = analogio.AnalogIn(board.A1)  # A1 on Trinket/Gemma boards
```

Understanding Resolution

The resolution of an ADC determines how many discrete levels it can measure. A 10-bit ADC can differentiate between 2^10 = 1024 levels, while a 12-bit ADC can distinguish between 2^12 = 4096 levels.

```python
# Reading and printing the raw value
value = adc.read_u16()  # Returns a 16-bit unsigned integer for 12-bit ADCs
print(value)
```

Wiring Potentiometers or Photocells in Voltage Dividers

Potentiometers (variable resistors) and photocells (light-dependent resistors) can be wired as voltage dividers to provide analog signals. Connect one end of the potentiometer or photocell to a power rail, the other end to ground, and read from the middle pin.

Reading Values and Mapping to Volts

To read an ADC value and map it to volts:

```python
# Reading voltage using a known reference voltage (e.g., 3.3V)
reference_voltage = 3.3
raw_value = adc.read_u16()
voltage = raw_value * (reference_voltage / (2**16 - 1))
print(f"{voltage:.2f} volts")
```

Example: LM35/TMP36 Temperature Conversion

The LM35 and TMP36 are popular temperature sensors that output an analog voltage proportional to the Celsius temperature. To read their values:

```python
# Reading temperature using LM35 or TMP36
reference_voltage = 3.3
raw_value = adc.read_u16()
```

```python
voltage = raw_value * (reference_voltage / (2**16 - 1))
temperature_celsius = voltage * 100  # For LM35, adjust for TMP36 if needed
print(f"{temperature_celsius:.2f} degrees Celsius")
```

Noise Reduction via Averaging

To reduce noise and improve measurement accuracy, you can take multiple readings and average them.

```python
# Average readings to reduce noise
num_readings = 10
total = 0
for _ in range(num_readings):
    total += adc.read_u16()
average_value = total / num_readings
print(f"Averaged value: {average_value}")
```

Using Analog Input to Control PWM (Potentiometer LED Dimmer)

Analog inputs can be used to control Pulse Width Modulation (PWM) signals, allowing you to create dimmable LEDs using a potentiometer.

```python
# Dimming an LED using a potentiometer on pin P0 (ADC)
import pulseio

pwm = pulseio.PWMOut(board.P13, frequency=4096, duty_cycle=0)

while True:
    raw_value = adc.read_u16()
    duty_cycle = int((raw_value / 2**16) * 65535)
    pwm.duty_cycle = duty_cycle
```

External ADC Chips (MCP3008) for Boards Without Built-in ADC

Some microcontrollers don't have built-in ADCs. In such cases, external ADC chips like the MCP3008 can be used.

```python
# Using an MCP3008 with MicroPython (BBC micro:bit)
import machine

spi = machine.SPI()
mcp = machine.ADC(spi, machine.Pin(26))  # Connect CS pin to P0 on BBC micro:bit

raw_value = mcp.read_u16()  # Read channel 0
voltage = raw_value * (3.3 / 2**16)
print(f"{voltage:.2f} volts")
```

With these examples, you should now be able to read analog signals using Python on embedded systems and process them for various applications like temperature measurement, light sensing, or controlling LED brightness.

Chapter 12: I²C Protocol and Interfacing I²C Sensors

This chapter introduces the Inter-Integrated Circuit (I²C) protocol, a popular method for interfacing embedded systems with various sensors and peripherals. We'll cover I²C fundamentals, initializing I²C communication, and demonstrate reading/writing to sensors using Python on platforms like the Raspberry Pi Pico and micro:bit.

I²C Fundamentals

I²C is a serial bus used for connecting low-speed peripherals to a single or multiple microcontrollers. It consists of two lines:

- **SDA (Serial Data Line)**: Used for data transmission.
- **SCL (Serial Clock Line)**: Provides the clock signal for data synchronization.

I²C uses a master-slave architecture where one device acts as the master, initiating communication and controlling the clock. Other devices act as slaves, responding to commands issued by the master.

Each slave has a unique 7-bit address used for identification during communication. Register-based communication is employed, allowing access to specific sensor or peripheral registers via read/write operations.

I²C requires pull-up resistors on both SDA and SCL lines. Typically, these are internal to the devices connected but can be external if necessary.

Initializing I²C Communication

In Python, we use the machine module for initializing I²C communication on microcontrollers like the RP2040 (Raspberry Pi Pico). For platforms with busio, such as the micro:bit, use that module instead. Here's how to initialize I²C:

RP2040 (Pico):

```python
import machine
```

```
sda = machine.Pin(0)
scl = machine.Pin(1)

i2c = machine.I2C(sda=sda, scl=scl, freq=100000)  # Initialize I²C with a frequency of
100kHz
```

micro:bit:

```
from microbit import *

# Initialize I²C with SDA on pin P0 and SCL on pin P1 at 400kHz
i2c = busio.I2C(P0, P1, freq=400000)
```

Scanning for Devices

To identify connected devices, scan the address range (0x08 to 0x77) and check if each address responds:

RP2040 (Pico):

```
for addr in range(0x08, 0x78):
    try:
        i2c.writeto(addr, b'\x01')  # Send a start byte to wake up the device
        print(f"Device found at address: {addr}")
    except OSError as e:
        if e.errno == 5:  # No such file or directory error indicates no device found
            continue
        else:
            raise
```

Reading/Writing Registers

Use readfrom_mem to read data from a register and writeto_mem to write data into a register:

RP2040 (Pico):

```
# Read humidity data from the HTU21D sensor at address 0x40
humidity_data = i2c.readfrom_mem(0x40, 0xF5, 3)  # Register address and bytes to
read


# Write a value (0x8E) into the CTRL_REG1 register of the LSM6DS3TR-C sensor at
address 0x6A
i2c.writeto_mem(0x6A, 0x20, b'\x8E')  # Register address and byte to write
```

Example: BME280 Temperature/Humidity/Pressure Sensor

Connect the BME280 sensor to your RP2040-based board:

- VCC to 3V3
- GND to ground
- SDA to GP0 (SDA)
- SCL to GP1 (SCL)

Initialize communication and read temperature, humidity, and pressure data:

```python
from bme280 import BME280

i2c = machine.I2C(sda=machine.Pin(0), scl=machine.Pin(1), freq=100000)
bme = BME280(mode=BME280.NORMAL, address=0x76, i2c=i2c)  # Address may
vary based on SDO/ADDR pin configuration

while True:
    temp, pres, hum = bme.read_compensated_data()
    print(f"Temperature: {temp/100:.2f}°C")
    print(f"Pressure: {pres/25600:.2f}hPa")
    print(f"Humidity: {hum/1024:.2f}%RH\n")
```

Interpreting Datasheets for Register Maps

To effectively communicate with an I²C sensor, consult its datasheet to understand the register map, addressing modes, and data formats. For example:

- BME280 datasheet: https://www.bosch-sensortec.com/cc/downloads/products/sensors/bme280/

Managing Multiple Devices or Using Multiplexers

When connecting multiple I²C devices, ensure they have unique addresses (by changing the ADDR/SDO pin configuration) to avoid conflicts. If address collisions occur, use multiplexers like the PCA9517 to manage multiple devices on a single bus:

Connect the PCA9517 as follows and control it via Python:

```python
import machine

sda = machine.Pin(0)
scl = machine.Pin(1)
mux_addr = 0x74  # PCA9517's I²C address

# Initialize I²C for the multiplexer
mux_i2c = machine.I2C(sda=sda, scl=scl, freq=100000)

def select_channel(channel):
    mux_i2c.writeto(mux_addr, bytes([channel & 0x0F]))  # Write channel number to select devices

# Use the selected channel for communicating with connected sensors
```

Chapter 13: SPI Protocol and Interfacing SPI Devices

SPI Basics

The Serial Peripheral Interface (SPI) is a high-speed, full-duplex communication protocol used for connecting microcontrollers to external peripherals like sensors, displays, and memory chips. The SPI bus consists of four lines:

- **Master Out Slave In (MOSI)**: Used by the master to send data to the slave.
- **Master In Slave Out (MISO)**: Used by the slave to send data back to the master.
- **Serial Clock (SCK)**: Generated by the master and used to synchronize data transfer between master and slave.
- **Chip Select (CS)**: Used by the master to select a specific slave device. Each slave has its own CS line.

SPI is a master-slave protocol where only one master controls data transmission. Slaves are selected via their respective CS lines, allowing multiple slaves to coexist on the same SPI bus.

Initializing SPI

In Python for Microcontrollers (PicoW), you can initialize an SPI bus using the machine library. Here's a simple example:

```
from machine import Pin, SPI


sck = Pin(2)
mosi = Pin(3)
miso = Pin(4)
cs = Pin(5)


spi = SPI(0, sck=sck, mosi=mosi, miso=miso)  # Initialize SPI bus on PicoW
```

In CircuitPython (e.g., ESP32), use the busio library:

```
from board import SCK, MOSI, MISO, D10
from busio import SPI

spi = SPI(sck=SCK, mosi=MOSI, miso=MISO)  # Initialize SPI bus on ESP32
```

Using Chip Select (CS)

The CS line is typically connected to a slave's chip enable pin. To select a specific slave device, set the corresponding CS pin low:

```
cs = Pin(5)
spi.select(cs)  # Select slave by setting CS low
```

After data transfer, deselect the slave by setting CS high:

```
spi.deselect()  # Deselect slave by setting CS high
```

Writing and Reading Data

To write data to a slave device, use spi.write():

```
data = bytearray([0xA5, 0xAA])  # Example data
spi.write(data)  # Write data to selected slave
```

To read data from a slave device, use spi.readinto() with a buffer:

```
buffer = bytearray(2)
spi.readinto(buffer)  # Read data into buffer
print(buffer)  # Display received data
```

Example: SPI OLED Display Driver

Let's connect an SSD1306 OLED display to our PicoW board and send some text using SPI:

```
from machine import Pin, SPI
from ssd1306 import SSD1306_I2C  # Import SSD1306 driver
```

```
sck = Pin(2)
mosi = Pin(3)
miso = Pin(4)
cs = Pin(5)

spi = SPI(0, sck=sck, mosi=mosi, miso=miso)  # Initialize SPI bus
display = SSD1306_I2C(128, 64, spi, cs)  # Create display object

display.text("Hello, SPI!", 0, 0, 1)  # Write text to display
display.show()  # Display updated content
```

Alternative: SPI ADC Example

You can also interface with SPI Analog-to-Digital Converters (ADC), like the ADS1115. Here's a simple example using the Adafruit ADS1115 library:

```
from machine import Pin, SPI
import adafruit_ads1x15.ads1115 as ADS
import time

sck = Pin(2)
mosi = Pin(3)
miso = Pin(4)
cs = Pin(5)

spi = SPI(0, sck=sck, mosi=mosi, miso=miso)  # Initialize SPI bus
ads = ADS.ADS1115(spi, cs)  # Create ADS1115 object

while True:
    conversion = ads.read_adc(0) / (2**15 - 1) * 3.3  # Read ADC value and convert to
voltage
```

```
print(f"Voltage: {conversion:.2f} V")  # Print voltage level
time.sleep(0.5)  # Wait for half a second before next reading
```

Matching Clock Polarity/Phase and Baud Rate

When interfacing with SPI devices, ensure you match the clock polarity (CPOL), clock phase (CPHA), and baud rate settings on your microcontroller with those of the external device. These settings can usually be configured when initializing the SPI bus:

```
spi = SPI(0, sck=sck, mosi=mosi, miso=miso, freq=1000000, polarity=1, phase=1)  #
Set frequency, CPOL, and CPHA
```

Trade-offs: SPI vs. I²C

Both SPI and I²C are popular communication protocols for embedded systems. Here's a brief comparison:

	SPI	I²C
Speed	High (up to 10 MHz)	Medium (up to 400 kHz)
Data Rate	Full-duplex	Half-duplex with clock stretching
Addressing	No addressing	Up to 1024 devices with 7-bit or 10-bit addressing
slaves per bus	Limited by CS lines	Many slaves can share the same bus

SPI is faster and supports full-duplex communication, making it suitable for high-speed data transfer between a master device and one or more slaves. However, SPI has limited scalability due to the need for separate CS lines for each slave.

I²C, on the other hand, offers better scalability with up to 1024 devices per bus but at the cost of slower data rates and half-duplex communication. I²C is often used when multiple slaves need to share the same bus, such as in sensor networks or display matrices.

In conclusion, choose SPI for high-speed data transfer between a master and few slaves, and use I²C when multiple slaves need to coexist on the same bus.

Chapter 14: Using Libraries and Drivers to Simplify Hardware Interaction

In the journey towards embedded systems development using Python, interacting with hardware can often seem daunting due to its low-level nature. However, high-level libraries can greatly simplify this process by abstracting away complex communication details. This chapter explores how to leverage libraries and drivers to interact with hardware more efficiently using Python on embedded systems.

Why Use Libraries?

High-level libraries provide several benefits:

1. **Abstraction**: They hide the complexity of low-level communication protocols, allowing you to focus on your application logic.
2. **Consistency**: Libraries offer a consistent interface for interacting with different hardware components.
3. **Community Support**: Many libraries are community-driven and well-documented, providing examples and troubleshooting assistance.

Popular Python Libraries for Embedded Systems

Adafruit CircuitPython

Adafruit's CircuitPython is a powerful platform built on MicroPython that makes it easy to code circuits using Python. It comes with a rich collection of libraries for various sensors, displays, and other hardware components. You can find the full list in the Adafruit Learn System.

micropython-lib

micropython-lib is an unofficial package index for MicroPython libraries. It hosts many community-contributed libraries for various sensors, modules, and platforms.

Installing Libraries on Device Filesystem

Before using a library in your embedded system project, you need to install it on the device's filesystem. Here's how you can do this:

1. **Copy the library file** (.py or .mpy) to your device using a method like:
   - Using a USB drive and copying files manually.
   - Utilizing a serial connection and tools like ampy or rshell.
2. **Place the library in the correct directory**. Libraries should be placed in the root directory (/lib/) for them to be accessible system-wide.

Example: Using an Accelerometer/IMU Library

Let's explore how to use a driver/library to interact with a sensor using Adafruit CircuitPython as an example. We'll use the LSM6DS33 accelerometer and gyroscope library.

First, install the library on your device by copying Adafruit_LSM6DS33.py to /lib/.

Now, create a Python script (main.py) with the following content:

```python
import board
import adafruit_lsm6ds33

# Create sensor object using the I2C bus
i2c = board.I2C()
sensor = adafruit_lsm6ds33.LSM6DS33(i2c)

while True:
    # Read acceleration and angular rate data
    x, y, z = sensor.acceleration
    rx, ry, rz = sensor.gyro

    print(f"Acceleration (m/s²): ({x:.2f}, {y:.2f}, {z:.2f})")
```

```
print(f"Angular Rate (rad/s): ({rx:.2f}, {ry:.2f}, {rz:.2f})\n")

# Sleep for 0.1s to reduce CPU usage
time.sleep(0.1)
```

This script reads acceleration and angular rate data from the LSM6DS33 sensor using the Adafruit library and prints it out.

OLED Display Library Workflow

To use an OLED display library like ssd1306, follow these steps:

1. Install the library on your device.
2. Import the library in your Python script (main.py).
3. Initialize the display by providing the correct I2C bus and reset pin (if required).

Here's a basic example using an SSD1306-based OLED display:

```
import board
import digitalio
import adafruit_ssd1306

# Define display reset pin
reset_pin = digitalio.DigitalInOut(board.OLED_RST)

# Create I2C object
i2c = board.I2C()

# Initialize display using the I2C bus and reset pin
display = adafruit_ssd1306.SSD1306_I2C(i2c, reset_pin)

# Show message on the display
display.message("Hello, World!\nFrom CircuitPython!")
```

GPIO Zero: One-Line Control on Raspberry Pi

GPIO Zero is a popular library for working with GPIO pins on Raspberry Pis. It simplifies controlling digital output pins as shown below:

```python
from gpiozero import LED
import time

# Define an LED object connected to pin 18 (BCM mode)
led = LED(18)

while True:
    # Turn the LED on for 0.5s
    led.on()
    time.sleep(0.5)

    # Turn the LED off for 0.5s
    led.off()
    time.sleep(0.5)
```

Memory Trade-offs vs. Direct Register Access

Using libraries often comes with memory trade-offs since they load additional code into your system. However, this trade-off is generally worth it due to the increased ease of use and reduced development time.

Alternatively, you can interact directly with hardware registers using direct register access methods like struct in Python. This approach reduces memory usage but increases complexity and development time:

```python
import busio
import struct

# Define I2C bus and sensor address
```

```python
i2c = busio.I2C(board.SCL, board.SDA)
addr = 0x6A


def read16(reg):
    # Read 16-bit value from given register address
    data = bytearray(3)
    data[0] = reg & 0xFF
    i2c.writeto(addr, data)
    time.sleep(0.01)
    i2c.readfrom_into(addr, data)
    return struct.unpack(">H", bytes(data[1:]))[0]


# Read acceleration data directly from registers
x = read16(0x28) / (1 << 16)
y = read16(0x2A) / (1 << 16)
z = read16(0x2C) / (1 << 16)


print(f"Acceleration (m/s²): ({x:.2f}, {y:.2f}, {z:.2f})")
```

Leveraging Community Resources

To focus more on application logic, leverage community resources like libraries, examples, and forums. Websites such as Adafruit Learn System, MicroPython forum, and GitHub repositories offer invaluable help and support for your embedded systems projects.

In the next chapter, we'll explore how to handle exceptions and errors in Python on embedded systems to create more robust applications.

Chapter 15: IoT Basics – Connecting Your Device to the Internet

This chapter introduces you to the world of the Internet of Things (IoT) and guides you through connecting your embedded systems to the internet using various modules and methods in Python. We'll explore hardware options, software libraries, and best practices for secure and efficient data communication.

IoT Overview

The Internet of Things (IoT) refers to the networking of physical objects—vehicles, home appliances, industrial equipment, sensors, etc.—embedded with electronics, software, and network connectivity, allowing them to collect and exchange data. Key IoT use cases include:

- **Remote Data Monitoring**: Collecting sensor data from remote locations and storing it in the cloud for analysis.
- **Control Systems**: Controlling devices remotely based on received commands or sensor feedback.

Hardware for Connectivity

Several modules enable your embedded systems to connect to the internet wirelessly. Here are two popular ones:

1. **ESP32/ESP8266**: These are low-cost Wi-Fi modules with built-in microcontrollers, supporting MicroPython and CircuitPython. They have extensive GPIO pins for connecting various sensors and actuators.

   Example: Connecting an ESP32 to your network using the network module in MicroPython:

   ```
   import network
   ```

```
sta_if = network.WLAN(network.STA_IF)
sta_if.active(True)
sta_if.connect('your_SSID', 'your_password')
```

2. **Bluetooth Low Energy (BLE) Modules**: Like HM-10 or CC2540, these modules allow your device to connect to smartphones or other BLE-enabled devices.

Wi-Fi Setup

To set up a Wi-Fi connection on your module, you'll need the following information:

- **SSID**: The name of your Wi-Fi network.
- **Password**: The password for your Wi-Fi network.

Here's how to set up Wi-Fi on ESP32/ESP8266 using MicroPython's network module:

```python
import network

# Create a WiFi interface object
sta_if = network.WLAN(network.STA_IF)

# Activate the interface (if not already activated)
sta_if.active(True)

# Connect to your Wi-Fi network
sta_if.connect('your_SSID', 'your_password')

# Wait for connection to succeed
while not sta_if.isconnected():
    pass

print(f'Connected on {sta_if.ifconfig()[0]}')
```

For CircuitPython using Adafruit's adafruit_requests library, Wi-Fi setup is similar but requires importing and configuring the wifi module:

```
import wifi
from adafruit_requests import session


# Initialize the network interface (e.g., ESP8266)
interface = wifi.WiFi()


# Connect to your Wi-Fi network
interface.connect('your_SSID', 'your_password')


while not interface.isconnected():
    pass


print(f'Connected on {interface.ifconfig()[0]}')
```

Raspberry Pi Networking

Raspberry Pis have built-in Wi-Fi and Ethernet connectivity. To use them with Python, you'll employ the socket module for low-level networking and requests for high-level HTTP requests.

Example: Sending an HTTP GET request using requests:

```
import requests


response = requests.get('http://api.example.com/data')
data = response.json()
print(data)
```

Testing Connectivity

Once connected to the internet, you can test your device's connectivity using ping or sending HTTP GET requests.

Example: Ping Google DNS server using socket:

```python
import socket

ip = '8.8.8.8'  # Google DNS IP address
port = 53

sock = socket.socket(socket.AF_INET, socket.SOCK_DGRAM)
sock.settimeout(1)

try:
    sock.sendto(b'ping', (ip, port))
    data, _ = sock.recvfrom(1024)
    print(f'SUCCESS: {data.decode()} from {ip}')
except socket.error as err:
    print(f'FAILURE: {err}')
```

Data and Memory Constraints

Small devices have limited processing power and memory. When designing IoT systems, consider:

- **Data Size**: Keep transmitted data small to minimize energy usage and network congestion.
- **Battery Life**: Optimize your device's sleep modes to extend battery life.

Security Basics

Securing your IoT device is crucial to protect user privacy and prevent unauthorized access. Here are some basics:

1. **Secure Credential Storage**: Store credentials (e.g., Wi-Fi passwords) securely using hardware security modules or encryption libraries like cryptography.

2. **HTTPS/MQTT over TLS**: Use secure communication protocols like HTTPS and MQTT with Transport Layer Security (TLS). In Python, use libraries such as ssl

for low-level TLS/SSL support or higher-level libraries like requests with cert verification enabled.

Example: Sending an HTTP GET request using HTTPS with certificate verification:

```python
import requests

response = requests.get('https://api.example.com/data', verify='/path/to/cert.pem')
data = response.json()
print(data)
```

In this chapter, we've explored the basics of connecting embedded systems to the internet and discussed essential considerations for designing secure and efficient IoT devices. In the next chapter, we'll delve deeper into data communication protocols like MQTT and CoAP.

Note: Always follow security best practices when working with IoT devices to protect user privacy and prevent unauthorized access or device tampering.

Chapter 16: IoT Communication Protocols - MQTT and HTTP

In this chapter, we'll explore two popular communication protocols used in Internet of Things (IoT) applications: Message Queuing Telemetry Transport (MQTT) and Hypertext Transfer Protocol (HTTP). We'll discuss their architectures, use cases, and demonstrate how to implement them using Python on embedded systems like the Raspberry Pi Pico.

MQTT Pub/Sub Model

MQTT is a lightweight publish/subscribe protocol designed for low bandwidth, high latency networks. It follows a simple broker-client architecture:

- **Broker**: The server that facilitates communication between clients.
- **Topics**: Clients publish messages to topics or subscribe to them to receive messages.
- **Quality of Service (QoS)**: MQTT supports three levels of QoS to ensure message delivery:
    - 0: At most once (fire and forget).
    - 1: At least once (acks with packet id).
    - 2: Exactly once (acks with packet id and waits for broker ack).

Setting up MQTT Client

We'll use the umqtt.simple library for MicroPython and adafruit_mqtt for CircuitPython to connect to an MQTT broker. First, install the required libraries:

```
pip install umqtt.simple  # For MicroPython
pip install adafruit-mqtt  # For CircuitPython
```

Publishing Sensor Data

Here's an example of publishing sensor data (DHT22 temperature and humidity) using umqtt.simple on a Raspberry Pi Pico:

```python
import uasyncio
from umqtt import simple as mqtt_simple
from machine import DHT22, Pin

# Initialize DHT22 sensor
dht = DHT22(Pin(15))

async def publish_sensor_data():
    client = mqtt_simple.MQTTClient('client_id', 'broker.hivemq.com')
    await client.connect()

    while True:
        dht.measure()
        temp, hum = dht.temperature(), dht.humidity()
        await client.publish('iot/sensors/dht22', f'Temperature: {temp}, Humidity: {hum}')
        await uasyncio.sleep(60)  # Publish every minute

    await client.disconnect()

uasyncio.run(publish_sensor_data())
```

Subscribing to Control Topics

Now, let's subscribe to a topic to receive control commands:

```python
from umqtt import MQTTClient

def on_message(topic, msg):
    print(f"Received message on {topic}: {msg.decode()}")
```

```
client = MQTTClient('client_id', 'broker.hivemq.com')
client.set_callback(on_message)
client.connect()
client.subscribe('iot/controls/led')

while True:
    client.wait_msg()

client.disconnect()
```

HTTP REST

HTTP is the foundation of data communication on the web. We'll use it for one-off data pushes and interacting with cloud IoT platforms.

POST/GET via urequests or adafruit_requests

Here's an example of sending a GET request using urequests:

```
import urequests

response = urequests.get('http://jsonplaceholder.typicode.com/todos/1')
data = response.json()
print(data)
```

And here's a POST request using adafruit_requests on CircuitPython:

```
from adafruit_requests import Session
import json

session = Session()
headers = {'Content-Type': 'application/json'}
data = {'key1': 'value1', 'key2': 'value2'}
```

```
response = session.post('http://your-server.com/endpoint', data=json.dumps(data),
headers=headers)
print(response.json())
```

Requests on Pi

For the Raspberry Pi, you can use the requests library:

```
import requests

response = requests.get('http://jsonplaceholder.typicode.com/todos/1')
data = response.json()
print(data)


data = {'key1': 'value1', 'key2': 'value2'}
headers = {'Content-Type': 'application/json'}
response = requests.post('http://your-server.com/endpoint', json=data,
headers=headers)
print(response.json())
```

MQTT vs HTTP Trade-offs

- **MQTT**:
    - Lightweight and efficient.
    - Supports bi-directional communication (pub/sub).
    - Requires a dedicated broker server.
    - Suitable for continuous telemetry.
- **HTTP**:
    - Widely supported, easy to set up.
    - Simple one-off data pushes.
    - Suitable for cloud IoT platforms and RESTful APIs.

Cloud IoT Platforms Integration

Cloud IoT platforms like AWS IoT and Adafruit IO provide managed services for IoT device management, data processing, and storage. To integrate with these platforms, you'll need to set up an account, create a new project/app, and follow the platform's guidelines to connect your MQTT or HTTP client.

In this chapter, we've covered the basics of MQTT and HTTP communication protocols in IoT applications. You now have the tools to implement publish/subscribe models with MQTT and one-off data pushes using HTTP on embedded systems running Python.

Chapter 17: IoT Project - Building a Simple Connected Sensor System

In this chapter, we'll build a simple connected sensor system using Python to collect temperature and humidity data from the BME280 or DHT22 sensor and publish it over Wi-Fi using MQTT. We'll also enable bidirectional communication to control an LED remotely. The hardware components required are:

- ESP32 or Pico W (Wi-Fi enabled microcontroller)
- BME280 or DHT22 (temperature/humidity sensor)
- Status LED
- Breadboard and necessary jumper wires

Project Overview

Our project will involve the following steps:

1. Initialize and periodically read temperature and humidity data from the sensor.
2. Implement averaging to improve measurement accuracy.
3. Connect to Wi-Fi on boot.
4. Publish sensor data using MQTT or HTTP.
5. Set up remote monitoring via a dashboard or HTTP endpoint.
6. Enable bidirectional communication to toggle LED status or change reading frequency remotely.
7. Ensure autorun of the code via main.py or code.py.
8. Test reconnection and implement error handling.

Hardware Setup

ESP32/Pico W and Sensor Pin Connections

For this project, we'll connect our sensor (BME280 or DHT22) to the ESP32/Pico W as follows:

- **VCC** and **GND** to the respective pins on the microcontroller.
- **SDA** (BME280) or **DATA** (DHT22) to one of the GPIO pins (e.g., 21).
- **SCL** (BME280) to another GPIO pin (e.g., 22).

For simplicity, we'll connect the status LED's **positive** leg (**Anode**) to a third GPIO pin (e.g., 5) and its negative leg (**Cathode**) to ground through a resistor (around 330 ohms).

Software Setup

Initialize Sensor and Periodic Reading

First, let's initialize our sensor and implement periodic reading. We'll use the Adafruit_BME280 library for BME280 or Adafruit_DHT for DHT22.

```
import machine
from bme280 import *
# or
# from dht import *

sensor = BME280(address=0x76, pin_mode=machine.Pin.OPEN_DRAIN)
# or
# sensor = DHT(pin=21)

def read_sensor():
    try:
        temp, humidity = sensor.read()
        return temp, humidity
    except OSError as e:
        print(f"Sensor read error: {e}")
```

To improve measurement accuracy, we'll implement averaging by taking several readings and calculating the mean.

```python
def average_readings(n=10):
    temps, humidities = [], []
    for _ in range(n):
        temp, humidity = read_sensor()
        temps.append(temp)
        humidities.append(humidity)
    return sum(temps) / len(temps), sum(humidities) / len(humidities)
```

Wi-Fi Connectivity on Boot

To connect to Wi-Fi on boot, we'll create a function that reads the credentials from an external file (credentials.json).

```python
import json


def load_credentials():
    with open('credentials.json') as f:
        return json.load(f)


def connect_wifi(credentials):
    import network

    station = network.WLAN(network.STA_IF)
    station.active(True)
    station.connect(credentials['ssid'], credentials['password'])
```

Publish Sensor Data using MQTT or HTTP

For MQTT, we'll use the umqtt.robust library to handle reconnection and errors gracefully.

```python
import uasyncio
from umqtt import robust
```

```python
def publish_mqtt(data, topic="sensor/data"):
    client = robust.RobustMQTT(broker="your_broker_ip", port=1883)
    async with client:
        await client.connect()
        await client.publish(topic, data)


# To use HTTP, you can adapt the following example to send POST requests using
# `uasyncio` and `urequests`.
```

Remote Monitoring via Dashboard or HTTP Endpoint

For remote monitoring, we'll set up a simple dashboard using a web framework like Bottle. This will allow us to display sensor data in real-time.

```python
from bottle import route, run


@route("/")
def home():
    temp, humidity = average_readings()
    return f"Temperature: {temp:.2f}°C<br>Humidity: {humidity:.2f}%"


run(host="0.0.0.0", port=80)
```

Bidirectional Communication

To enable bidirectional communication, we'll add additional topics to our MQTT broker for controlling the LED remotely.

```python
@asyncio.coroutine
def handle_mqtt_message(topic, message):
    if topic == "led/command":
        command = int(message.decode())
        led.value(command)
```

```
# In your main loop:
client.on_message(handle_mqtt_message)
```

Autorun Code via main.py/code.py

To autorun our code on boot, we'll simply place it in the main.py or code.py file (depending on your microcontroller) and power up the board.

```
# main.py or code.py
import your_script

your_script.main()
```

Testing Reconnection and Error Handling

To test reconnection and implement error handling, we'll use a try-except block around our network connections and sensor readings. For MQTT, we'll use the umqtt library's built-in error handling.

```
while True:
    try:
        connect_wifi(load_credentials())
    except OSError as e:
        print(f"Wi-Fi connection error: {e}")
        continue

    # ... rest of your code ...
```

Use Cases and Extension Ideas

Some use cases and extension ideas for this project include:

- Implementing low-power mode to conserve energy.
- Adding support for multiple sensors and publishing their data separately.

- Creating a simple alarm system that triggers when temperature/humidity thresholds are exceeded.
- Integrating with other smart home devices using MQTT or HTTP.

Chapter 18: Robotics Basics - Motors, Movement, and Sensor Integration

Embedded systems often interact with the physical world through motors and sensors. This chapter introduces the basics of robotics using Python for embedded systems, focusing on actuators (motors), motor drivers, sensor integration, and control loops.

Actuators: Motors and Their Uses

DC Motors

DC motors are simple, widely used, and suitable for continuous rotation tasks like driving wheels in robots. They have two terminals and rotate continuously when powered. Typical uses include robot wheels, drills, and fans.

Servo Motors

Servo motors can rotate to a specific angle (within their range) with great precision. They're perfect for tasks requiring accurate positioning like robot arms or steering mechanisms. Servos have three terminals: power (VCC), ground (GND), and control (SIG).

Stepper Motors

Stepper motors divide a full rotation into smaller steps, allowing precise position control without feedback sensors. They're ideal for applications needing exact positioning like CNC machines or robotic arms. Steppers require more complex control circuits than DC motors.

Motor Drivers

Actuators need motor drivers to interface with microcontrollers. H-bridge chips (e.g., L293D) are common motor driver modules that allow bidirectional control of DC and stepper motors using GPIO pins. They use PWM signals for speed control and can connect directly to a Raspberry Pi's GPIO pins.

Motor Control with Python

Controlling DC Motors

To control a DC motor connected via an H-bridge chip, you can use the gpiozero library in Python:

```python
from gpiozero import Robot
from time import sleep

# Initialize robot with left and right wheel pins
robot = Robot(left=24, right=23)

try:
    # Move robot forward for 1 second
    robot.forward()
    sleep(1)
finally:
    # Stop robot on exit
    robot.stop()
```

Controlling Servo Motors

For servo motor control, you can use the CircuitPython library's Servo class:

```python
from board import *
import time
import pulseio

# Initialize servo with PWM pin and frequency
servo = pulseio.PWMOut(SERVO_PIN, freq=50)

while True:
    # Set servo angle between 0° - 180°
```

```
    servo.duty_cycle = 65536 * (angle / 180)
    time.sleep(0.1)
```

Sensor Integration

Ultrasonic Sensors

Ultrasonic sensors measure distances by sending out sound waves and listening for echoes. The ultrasonic module in Python can be used to read distance measurements:

```python
from ultrasonic import SRF05
import time

# Initialize ultrasonic sensor with trigger/echo pins
sensor = SRF05(TRIG_PIN, ECHO_PIN)

while True:
    # Measure distance and print result (in cm)
    print("Distance: {:.2f}cm".format(sensor.distance))
    time.sleep(0.1)
```

Obstacle Avoidance Logic

Tying sensor data to motor control allows robots to avoid obstacles:

```python
while True:
    distance = sensor.distance

    if distance < OBSTACLE_THRESHOLD:
        # If obstacle detected, stop and reverse robot briefly
        robot.stop()
        time.sleep(0.2)
        robot.backward()
        time.sleep(0.1)
    else:
```

```
    # Otherwise, move forward
    robot.forward()
```

Power Supply Considerations

Motors require more power than logic circuits, so separate power rails are essential to prevent voltage drops and noise interference. Connect motors directly to their dedicated power source (e.g., batteries or a dedicated voltage regulator), while keeping logic circuits connected to the main board's power supply.

Continuous Control Loops

Robots often require continuous feedback loops for smooth operation. State machines can help manage complex robot behaviors, allowing transitions between states based on sensor inputs:

```python
from state_machine import *

# Define robot states and transitions
robot_states = {
    'IDLE': lambda: set(['FORWARD', 'TURNAROUND']),
    'FORWARD': lambda: set(['DETECT_OBSTACLE', 'IDLE']),
    'DETECT_OBSTACLE': lambda: set(['AVOID_OBSTACLE', 'FORWARD']),
    # Add more states and transitions as needed
}

# Initialize state machine with initial state
robot = StateMachine(robot_states, 'IDLE')

while True:
    robot.run()
```

In this chapter, we've covered the basics of actuators, motor drivers, sensor integration, and control loops for embedded systems using Python. By following these principles, you can create robots that interact effectively with their environment.

Chapter 19: Robotics Project - Building a Simple Robot with Python

Project Overview

In this chapter, we'll build a simple two-wheeled differential drive rover using Python. This robot will navigate using two DC gear motors and avoid obstacles using ultrasonic or IR sensors. We'll also implement line following behavior as an optional feature.

Components: - Controller (Raspberry Pi) - Two DC gear motors - Motor driver (L293D) - Caster wheel(s) - Ultrasonic/IR sensor(s) (e.g., HC-SR04, QRE11GR) - Battery pack (Li-ion battery or 9V battery with voltage regulator) - Mechanical assembly and wiring diagram

Python Movement Functions

First, let's define functions for moving the robot forward, backward, and turning using the RPi.GPIO library:

```python
import RPi.GPIO as GPIO
import time

# Initialize GPIO pins
GPIO.setmode(GPIO.BCM)
GPIO.setup([M1A, M1B], GPIO.OUT)  # Left motor
GPIO.setup([M2A, M2B], GPIO.OUT)  # Right motor

def forward(speed):
    left_speed = speed
    right_speed = speed
    set_motor_speeds(left_speed, right_speed)

def backward(speed):
```

```python
    left_speed = -speed
    right_speed = -speed
    set_motor_speeds(left_speed, right_speed)


def turn_left(speed):
    left_speed = speed * 0.5
    right_speed = -speed * 0.5
    set_motor_speeds(left_speed, right_speed)


def turn_right(speed):
    left_speed = -speed * 0.5
    right_speed = speed * 0.5
    set_motor_speeds(left_speed, right_speed)


def set_motor_speeds(left_speed, right_speed):
    GPIO.output(M1A, left_speed > 0)
    GPIO.output(M1B, left_speed < 0)
    GPIO.output(M2A, right_speed > 0)
    GPIO.output(M2B, right_speed < 0)


def stop():
    set_motor_speeds(0, 0)
```

Sensor Reading for Obstacle Avoidance

Now let's implement obstacle avoidance using the HC-SR04 ultrasonic sensor:

```python
import time


TRIG = 23
ECHO = 24
```

```python
def setup_ultrasonic():
    GPIO.setup(TRIG, GPIO.OUT)
    GPIO.setup(ECHO, GPIO.IN)

def get_distance():
    GPIO.output(TRIG, True)
    time.sleep(0.00001)
    GPIO.output(TRIG, False)

    while GPIO.input(ECHO) == 0:
        pulse_start = time.time()

    while GPIO.input(ECHO) == 1:
        pulse_end = time.time()

    pulse_duration = pulse_end - pulse_start
    distance = pulse_duration * 17150
    return distance

def obstacle_avoidance():
    setup_ultrasonic()
    while True:
        if get_distance() < 20:  # Adjust the threshold as needed
            turn_left(50)
            time.sleep(0.3)
        else:
            forward(50)
```

Line Following Behavior

For line following, we'll use the QRE11GR IR sensor:

```python
LF = 17  # Left photodiode
RF = 18  # Right photodiode


def setup_line_follow():
    GPIO.setup(LF, GPIO.IN)
    GPIO.setup(RF, GPIO.IN)


def line_following(speed):
    left_value = GPIO.input(LF)
    right_value = GPIO.input(RF)


    if left_value == 1 and right_value == 0:  # Left black, Right white - Turn right
        turn_right(speed)
    elif left_value == 0 and right_value == 1:  # Left white, Right black - Turn left
        turn_left(speed)
    else:
        forward(speed)  # Both on same color - Go straight
```

Main Loop Combining Behaviors

Next, we'll combine these behaviors with priority for obstacle avoidance in the main loop:

```python
def main():
    try:
        while True:
            obstacle_avoidance()
            line_following(50)
    except KeyboardInterrupt:
        GPIO.cleanup()
```

```
if __name__ == "__main__":
    main()
```

Optional Remote Tuning

For optional remote tuning via potentiometer or serial/Wi-Fi, you can add analog reading or serial communication to adjust the robot's speed and behavior parameters in real-time.

Field Testing and Parameter Tuning

After assembling and wiring your rover, test it on different surfaces like carpet, tile, and hardwood. Tune sensor thresholds, motor speeds, and turning rates to optimize performance for each surface.

Reflection on Python's Rapid Logic Development and Performance Limits

Python allows rapid prototyping and logic development due to its simplicity and extensive libraries. However, real-time performance might be limited compared to lower-level languages like C or C++. When optimizing performance, consider using native extensions or alternative microcontrollers with more powerful hardware.

In the next chapter, we'll explore advanced topics such as advanced sensor fusion techniques, autonomous navigation algorithms, and integrating more complex sensors like cameras for robot vision.

Advanced Topics: Multitasking, Interrupts, and Optimization

In this chapter, we delve into advanced topics crucial for embedded systems programming using Python. We'll explore concurrency challenges, hardware interrupts, cooperative multitasking, threading, real-time limitations, code optimization, memory management, and task offloading.

Concurrency Challenges in Single-Loop Code

In single-loop code, blocking I/O operations can lead to frozen inputs/outputs. To handle this, we use non-blocking I/O operations or implement cooperative multitasking.

Example: Using asyncio for non-blocking I/O with GPIO input.

```python
import asyncio
from pin import Pin


async def button_press(pin):
    while True:
        if pin.value == 0:  # Button pressed
            print("Button pressed!")
            await asyncio.sleep(0.1)  # Debounce delay


button = Pin(23, Pin.IN)
loop = asyncio.get_event_loop()
loop.run_until_complete(button_press(button))
```

Hardware Interrupts with Pin.irq() and Handler Constraints

Hardware interrupts allow event-driven code execution when a specific condition is met.

Example: Using Pin.irq for an interrupt-driven LED blink.

```python
from pin import Pin
import time


led = Pin(25, Pin.OUT)
button = Pin(23, Pin.IN, Pull.DOWN)
```

```
def button_pressed(pin):
    led.toggle()
    print("Button pressed!")


button.irq(trigger=Pin.IRQ_FALLING | Pin.IRQ_RISING, handler=button_pressed)


while True:
    time.sleep(1)  # Keep the program running
```

Constraints: Interrupt handlers should be short to minimize context switching overhead.

Cooperative Multitasking with uasyncio/asyncio

Cooperative multitasking allows multiple tasks to run concurrently without preemptive scheduling. We use await and async keywords for cooperative task yielding.

Example: Implementing a simple concurrent LED blinking using asyncio.

```
from pin import Pin
import asyncio


led1 = Pin(25, Pin.OUT)
led2 = Pin(12, Pin.OUT)


async def blink_led(led):
    while True:
        led.toggle()
        await asyncio.sleep(0.5)


async def main():
    task1 = asyncio.create_task(blink_led(led1))
    task2 = asyncio.create_task(blink_led(led2))
    await asyncio.gather(task1, task2)
```

```
loop = asyncio.get_event_loop()
loop.run_until_complete(main())
```

Python Threading on Pi and GIL Considerations

Python's Global Interpreter Lock (GIL) allows only one native thread to execute at a time. For concurrent I/O-bound tasks on the Raspberry Pi, threading can be beneficial.

Example: Using threads for simultaneous LED blinking and button detection.

```python
from pin import Pin
import threading
import time


led1 = Pin(25, Pin.OUT)
button = Pin(23, Pin.IN)


def blink_led():
    while True:
        led1.toggle()
        time.sleep(0.5)


def check_button():
    while True:
        if button.value == 0:  # Button pressed
            print("Button pressed!")
            time.sleep(0.1)  # Debounce delay


t1 = threading.Thread(target=blink_led)
t2 = threading.Thread(target=check_button)


t1.start()
```

```
t2.start()

t1.join()
t2.join()
```

GIL Considerations: For CPU-bound tasks, use multiprocessing instead of threading.

Real-time Limitations and Hardware Peripherals

Python's real-time limitations arise from its high-level nature. For critical tasks requiring deterministic execution times, consider using hardware peripherals or RTOS.

Example: Using a direct memory access (DMA) controller for fast data transfers.

```python
from machine import DMA, Pin

dma = DMA(0)
pin = Pin(25, Pin.OUT)

def dma_handler():
    pin.toggle()

dma.callback(dma_handler)
```

Code Optimization Techniques

Optimize Python code by minimizing allocations, using integer math, lookup tables, and built-in C functions for speed.

Example: Integer math for faster computation.

```python
# Faster integer division than float division
x = 10
y = 3
print(x // y)  # 3
```

```python
# Use built-in min() and max() for comparisons
a, b = 5, 7
print(max(a, b))  # 7
```

Memory Management with gc.collect() and Pre-allocation Buffers

Managing memory efficiently is crucial in embedded systems.

Example: Using gc.collect() to manually trigger garbage collection.

```python
import gc

# Allocate large objects
large_objects = [bytearray(1024 * 1024) for _ in range(5)]

print("Before GC: Memory used:", gc.mem_get_free())
gc.collect()
print("After GC: Memory used:", gc.mem_get_free())
```

Pre-allocating buffers: Allocate large memory blocks once and reuse them.

```python
buffer = bytearray(1024 * 1024)
# ... use buffer ...
```

Frozen Bytecode for Reducing Memory Usage

Frozen bytecode reduces memory usage by packaging the Python interpreter with your code into a single file (.mpy).

Example: Creating and running frozen bytecode.

```python
from micropython import const, opt_level
opt_level(0)  # Set optimization level to 0 (disable optimizations)
```

```
led = Pin(25, Pin.OUT)
while True:
    led.toggle()
    time.sleep(1)
```

RTOS or Multicore Offloading for Complex Tasks

For complex tasks requiring real-time guarantees or leveraging multicore processors, consider using an RTOS or offloading tasks to other cores.

Example: Using FreeRTOS on the Raspberry Pi Pico.

```
from machine import freq, reset
import time


freq(125_000_000)  # Set CPU frequency to 125 MHz


# Initialize FreeRTOS and create tasks...


reset()  # Reset the board to start FreeRTOS scheduler
```

In this chapter, we've explored advanced topics crucial for embedded systems programming using Python. By understanding these concepts, you'll be better equipped to handle complex tasks and optimize your code for performance and memory usage.

Chapter 21: Power Management and Low-Power Operation

Embedded systems often run on limited power sources like batteries. Efficient power management is crucial to maximize battery life and reduce heat generation. This chapter explores power management techniques for embedded systems using Python, focusing on MicroPython running on ESP32 or other compatible microcontrollers (MCUs).

Importance of Low-Power Design

Low-power design is essential for:

1. **Extended Battery Life**: Batteries have a limited capacity. Reducing current draw extends the time between charges.
2. **Heat Reduction**: Power consumption generates heat. Lower power usage keeps the system cooler, improving reliability and lifespan.

Measuring Current Draw

Measuring current draw helps identify power-hungry components and optimize power management strategies. Using an ammeter or a current sensor like the ACS712, you can monitor current in real-time. Here's a simple example using MicroPython on ESP32:

```python
from machine import ADC, Pin
import utime

# Connect ACS712 to ADC pin (e.g., A0)
adc = ADC(Pin(36))

def measure_current():
    # ACS712 sensitivity is 185mV/A
    VCC = 3.3
```

```python
    sensitivity = 185 / 1000
    current_Reading = adc.read_u16() * (VCC / 65535)
    current_mA = current_Reading / sensitivity
    return current_mA


while True:
    print(f"Current draw: {measure_current()} mA")
    utime.sleep(1)  # Adjust sleep duration based on desired sampling rate
```

MCU Sleep Modes

MCUs can enter various sleep modes to reduce power consumption. ESP32 has several sleep modes, including light and deep sleep.

Light Sleep

In light sleep mode (machine.lightsleep()), the CPU clock stops, reducing active current draw. However, peripherals like Wi-Fi and Bluetooth remain powered:

```python
import machine
import utime


while True:
    print("Going to light sleep...")
    machine.lightsleep()
```

Deep Sleep via machine.deepsleep()

Deep sleep mode (machine.deepsleep()) powers off most components, including peripherals. It consumes very little power but requires more wake-up time than light sleep:

```python
import machine
import utime
```

```python
def deepsleep_wake(awake, asleep):
    while True:
        print("Going to deep sleep...")
        machine.deepsleep(asleep * 1000)  # Convert seconds to milliseconds
        print("Woke up!")
        utime.sleep(awake)


# Deep sleep for 5 seconds, awake for 2 seconds
deepsleep_wake(2, 5)
```

Deep-Sleep Cycle Example

A common use case is periodic wake-read-sleep cycles. Here's an example using a DHT22 temperature sensor:

```python
import machine
from dht import DHT22
import utime


d = DHT22(machine.Pin(4))


while True:
    print("Waking up...")
    d.measure()
    print(f"Temperature: {d.temperature()}*C, Humidity: {d.humidity()}%")
    print("Going to deep sleep...")
    machine.deepsleep(60 * 1000)  # Deep sleep for 60 seconds
```

Light Sleep and Radio Off Strategies

To minimize power consumption:

1. **Disable unnecessary peripherals**: Turn off Wi-Fi, Bluetooth, and other radios when not in use.

2. **Use light sleep strategically**: Enter light sleep mode after short periods of activity to minimize wake-up time.

```python
import machine
import utime
from esp import raw

# Disable Wi-Fi and turn off antenna power
raw.wifi_power_off()
raw.pin_antenna(machine.Pin(5), False)

while True:
    print("Waking up...")
    utime.sleep(1)
    print("Going to light sleep...")
    machine.lightsleep()
```

Peripheral Power Gating with GPIO

Power gating involves disconnecting unused peripherals from the power source. On ESP32, you can use GPIO pins to enable/disable power to sensors or other peripherals:

```python
import machine
import utime

# Connect sensor VCC to GPIO19
power_pin = machine.Pin(19, machine.Pin.OUT)

while True:
    print("Powering up...")
    power_pin.on()
    utime.sleep(5)
    print("Powering down...")
```

```
power_pin.off()
utime.sleep(5)
```

Sensor Low-Power Modes

Many sensors have low-power modes. For example, the BME280 temperature and pressure sensor has a forced mode that reduces current draw:

```python
from machine import Pin, I2C
import bme280
import utime

i2c = I2C(scl=Pin(22), sda=Pin(21))
bme = bme280.BME280(address=0x76, i2c=i2c)
bme.init()

while True:
    print("Waking up...")
    bme.read_pressure()
    print(f"Pressure: {bme.pressure} Pa")
    print("Going to light sleep...")
    machine.lightsleep()
```

Raspberry Pi vs MCU Sleep

Raspberry Pi doesn't have built-in sleep modes like ESP32. To achieve low-power operation, you can:

1. **Disable unnecessary interfaces**: Turn off unused USB ports and disable unnecessary services.

2. **Shutdown the system**: Use shutdown command to power down the Raspberry Pi:

```bash
# Disable unused interfaces
echo "dtoverlay=disable-bt" | sudo tee -a /boot/config.txt
```

```
echo "dtoverlay=pi3-mini-wp" | sudo tee -a /boot/config.txt

# Shutdown command
sudo shutdown -h now
```

Duty Cycling and Batching Data in Code

Duty cycling involves periodically turning on/off devices to save power. Batching data involves processing multiple readings at once before entering sleep mode:

```python
import machine
from dht import DHT22
import utime

d = DHT22(machine.Pin(4))
data_batch = []

while True:
    print("Waking up...")
    for _ in range(10):
        d.measure()
        data_batch.append((d.temperature(), d.humidity()))
    print(f"Collected {len(data_batch)} readings")
    utime.sleep(60)  # Deep sleep for 60 seconds
```

Battery Selection and Regulator Efficiency

Battery selection depends on your power requirements:

- **Li-Ion**: High capacity, suitable for high-power applications.
- **AA/AAA batteries**: Low capacity but widely available. Use a boost converter to maintain stable voltage.
- **Coin cells**: Small size with limited capacity.

Regulator efficiency varies:

- **Buck converters** reduce voltage and can achieve high efficiencies (~90%).
- **Linear regulators** are simpler but less efficient (~30-50%).

Chapter 22: Deploying and Maintaining Embedded Python Projects

Now that you've created your embedded project using MicroPython, CircuitPython, or Python on a Raspberry Pi, it's time to explore how to deploy and maintain these systems in the real world. This chapter covers various aspects of deploying, updating, monitoring, and maintaining your projects, ensuring they run smoothly and securely.

Autorun on Boot

To ensure your project runs automatically upon booting up, you need to understand the boot sequence for different platforms:

- **MicroPython**: Use boot.py for running code at startup. If main.py is present, it will be executed afterward.

```
# boot.py
import machine
led = machine.Pin(25, machine.Pin.OUT)
led.on()  # Turn on LED at startup
```

- **CircuitPython**: The code.py file will autorun upon booting the board.

```
# code.py
import board
led = digitalio.DigitalInOut(board.LED)
led.direction = digitalio.Direction.OUT
led.value = True  # Turn on LED at startup
```

- **Raspberry Pi**: For Raspbian Lite, use systemd services or cron jobs to autorun your Python scripts.

```
# /etc/systemd/system/myscript.service
[Unit]
Description=My Script
```

```
[Service]
ExecStart=/usr/bin/python3 /home/pi/myscript.py


[Install]
WantedBy=multi-user.target
```

Prototype to Product: Transition Techniques

As your project evolves from prototype to product, consider the following transition techniques:

1. **Perfboard**: Start with perfboards for rapid prototyping.
2. **PCB Design**:
   - Use design software like Eagle, KiCad, or EasyEDA.
   - Consider factors such as component placement, trace width, and via size.
3. **Enclosure Techniques**:
   - 3D print custom enclosures.
   - Use off-the-shelf cases with appropriate modifications.

Over-The-Air (OTA) Updates vs Physical Updates

OTA updates allow your embedded devices to update wirelessly. In MicroPython, you can use the upip tool for OTA updating:

```python
import upip
upip.install('your_package')  # Update a package
upip.list()  # List installed packages
```

For physical updates, use methods such as SD card swapping (Raspberry Pi) or USB bootloading (CircuitPython boards).

Logging and Fault Tolerance

Use Python's built-in logging module to monitor your project:

```
import logging
logging.basicConfig(level=logging.INFO)
logging.info('This is an info message')
```

Implement try/except blocks for error handling and use the machine.WDT (watchdog timer) module in MicroPython to prevent system freezes:

```
try:
    # Critical code block
    pass
except Exception as e:
    logging.error(f'An error occurred: {e}')
finally:
    machine.wdt.feed()  # Feed watchdog timer
```

Secure Deployment

Ensure secure deployment by:

- **Updating credentials/keys**: Store sensitive data like passwords and keys securely using secure hardware modules or encrypted storage.
- **Disabling REPL (Read-Eval-Print Loop)**: Set REPL = False in your script to disable remote access for security reasons.
- **Safe Mode**: Run your project in safe mode (main.py -s) to prevent accidental changes during runtime.

Fleet Monitoring

Monitor your fleet of devices by implementing heartbeat functionality:

```
import ubinascii, machine
device_id = ubinascii.hexlify(machine.unique_id()).decode()  # Generate unique ID
```

Send heartbeats via MQTT or other protocols to a central server for monitoring.

Battery Maintenance and Solar Charging

For battery-powered devices:

1. **Monitor battery level**: Use appropriate libraries (e.g., machine.I2C for ADC communication) to monitor battery voltage.
2. **Implement power-saving techniques**: Reduce CPU clock speed, enable sleep modes (machine.deepsleep()), and minimize wireless communications.

Documentation for Users

Create comprehensive documentation explaining:

- Setup instructions
- Indicators and LEDs explanation
- Troubleshooting steps

By following these guidelines, you'll be well-equipped to deploy and maintain your embedded Python projects successfully.

Chapter 23: Python vs. C/C++ in Embedded Systems – Trade-offs and Integration

In this chapter, we explore the trade-offs and integration aspects of using Python versus C/C++ for embedded systems development.

Performance

When it comes to performance, compiled languages like C and C++ generally outperform interpreted languages such as Python. This is due to the way they are executed:

- **C/C++**: These languages are compiled into machine code, which is directly executed by the processor. As a result, they can achieve high speeds, even on relatively low-end microcontrollers.
    - *Example*: A simple 'Hello, World!' program in C might run at around 80 MHz on an embedded system.
- **Python**: Python is an interpreted language, meaning it's translated into bytecode which is then executed by a virtual machine. This introduces overhead and results in slower performance compared to native code.
    - *Example*: The same 'Hello, World!' program might run at around 800 MHz on MicroPython, which is significantly slower.

Here's a simple performance comparison:

```python
# Python (MicroPython)
import utime

start = utime.ticks_ms()
for _ in range(1_000_000):
    pass
print(f"Python time: {utime.ticks_diff(utime.ticks_ms(), start)} ms")
```

```
// C (on an 8-bit microcontroller like the ESP8266)
#include <esp_log.h>

portTickType start;
start = xTaskGetTickCount();

while (true) {
    // Do nothing
}

ESP_LOGI("C", "C time: %d ms", (xTaskGetTickCount() - start));
```

Memory Footprint

Memory usage is another critical factor in embedded systems:

- **Python**: Python's high-level nature and extensive standard library come at the cost of larger memory footprint. The Python runtime, along with its garbage collector, can consume a significant amount of RAM.
  - *Example*: MicroPython's memory usage is around 512 KB for its default configuration.
- **C/C++**: These languages offer more control over memory management, allowing developers to create lean binaries with minimal memory overhead.
  - *Example*: A 'Hello, World!' program in C might only consume a few kilobytes of RAM.

Here's a comparison of memory usage:

```
# Python (MicroPython)
import gc

gc.mem_alloc()
```

```
// C (using malloc.h for demonstration purposes, not actual size)
#include <malloc.h>

size_t mem_size = mallinfo().uordblks;
printf("C memory: %zu bytes\n", mem_size);
```

Real-time Control Granularity and Garbage Collection Overhead

Real-time control in embedded systems often requires precise timing and minimal overhead:

- **C/C++**: These languages offer fine-grained control over system resources, allowing developers to implement real-time systems with predictable behavior.
  - *Example*: Using FreeRTOS, developers can create tasks and queues with precise timing.

```
// C (using FreeRTOS)
#include "freertos/FreeRTOS.h"
#include "freertos/task.h"

void task_code(void* pvParameters) {
  while (true) {
    vTaskDelay(10 / portTICK_PERIOD_MS);
  }
}

void app_main() {
  xTaskCreate(&task_code, "task", 2048, NULL, 5, NULL);
}
```

- **Python**: Python's garbage collector can introduce overhead and unpredictable behavior in real-time systems due to its non-deterministic nature.

> – *Example*: Disabling the garbage collector might be necessary for real-time applications using MicroPython.

```
# Python (MicroPython)
import gc

gc.disable()  # Disable garbage collection for real-time tasks
```

Rapid Prototyping and High-level Libraries

Python offers several advantages for rapid prototyping:

- **Rapid Prototyping**: Python's simplicity allows developers to write code quickly, enabling faster prototyping of embedded systems.

```
# Python (MicroPython)
print("Hello, World!")
```

- **High-level Libraries**: Python has a vast ecosystem of libraries like NumPy, SciPy, and Matplotlib for scientific computing, data analysis, and visualization. These can significantly speed up development time.
  - *Example*: Using NumPy for matrix operations allows developers to write concise code that would otherwise require manual looping in C/C++.

```
# Python (NumPy)
import numpy as np

a = np.array([1, 2, 3])
b = np.array([4, 5, 6])
c = a + b
print(c)  # Output: [5 7 9]
```

Hardware SDKs and Integration with C/C++

Hardware SDKs for embedded systems are often provided in C or C++, allowing developers to interface directly with hardware peripherals:

- **C/C++**: Most hardware SDKs and drivers are written in C or C++. Integrating these into Python projects can be challenging due to language barriers.

```
// C (using an STM32CubeMX generated project)
HAL_GPIO_TogglePin(GPIOA, GPIO_PIN_5);
```

- **Python**: To integrate with C/C++ hardware SDKs, developers often need to use tools like ctypes or cffi. Alternatively, they can create native extensions using Python's C API.

```python
# Python (using ctypes)
import ctypes

lib = ctypes.CDLL('my_hardware_sdk.so')
lib.HAL_GPIO_TogglePin(0x40020014, 32)  # Toggle PA5 on an STM32F1xx board
```

Readability and Maintainability in Python

Python's readability and maintainability make it an excellent choice for embedded systems projects with a focus on software sustainability:

```python
# Python (MicroPython)
def blink_led(pin, delay_ms):
    while True:
        pin.value(not pin.value())
        utime.sleep_ms(delay_ms)


blink_led(Pin("LED", Pin.OUT), 500)
```

C/C++ for Constrained or Real-time Tasks

When performance, memory usage, or real-time behavior are critical, developers should consider using C or C++. For embedded systems with constrained resources, C is often the best choice due to its minimalistic nature and fine-grained control over system resources.

```
// C (blinking an LED on a microcontroller)
#define LED_PIN GPIO_PIN_5
#define LED_PORT GPIOC

void setup() {
    GPIO_InitTypeDef GPIO_InitStruct = {0};
    __HAL_RCC_GPIOC_CLK_ENABLE();
    GPIO_InitStruct.Pin = LED_PIN;
    GPIO_InitStruct.Mode = GPIO_MODE_OUTPUT_PP;
    GPIO_InitStruct.Pull = GPIO_NOPULL;
    GPIO_InitStruct.Speed = GPIO_SPEED_FREQ_LOW;
    HAL_GPIO_Init(LED_PORT, &GPIO_InitStruct);
}

void loop() {
    HAL_GPIO_TogglePin(LED_PORT, LED_PIN);
    HAL_Delay(500);
}
```

Hybrid Approach: Native C Modules or Viper in MicroPython for Hotspots

For performance-critical sections of code, developers can use a hybrid approach by implementing them in C/C++ and integrating with Python using tools like ctypes, cffi, or even using MicroPython's built-in support for native extensions (Viper).

```
# Python (using Viper for a performance-critical function)
@micropython.viper
def fast_sort(arr):
    # Implementation of the quicksort algorithm in Viper
    pass
```

```
arr = [3, 1, 4, 1, 5, 9]
fast_sort(arr)
print(arr)  # Output: [1, 1, 3, 4, 5, 9]
```

By combining Python's rapid prototyping and high-level libraries with C/C++'s performance and fine-grained control over system resources, developers can create efficient and maintainable embedded systems.

Conclusion and Next Steps in the Embedded Python Journey

Recap: From Basics to IoT and Robotics

You've come a long way since starting your journey into embedded systems using Python! You've explored MicroPython and CircuitPython, understood how to work with hardware like LEDs, sensors, and actuators, and even delved into Internet of Things (IoT) projects and robotics. Here's a quick recap:

- **Hardware Interfacing**: You learned how to control LEDs, read sensor data, and interact with buttons and switches.

  ```
  from machine import Pin
  led = Pin(25, Pin.OUT)
  led.on()  # Turn on the LED connected to GPIO25
  ```

- **IoT Projects**: You explored how to connect your embedded device to the internet using Wi-Fi or other networks and send/receive data.

  ```
  import network
  wlan = network.WLAN(network.STA_IF)
  wlan.active(True)
  wlan.connect('your_wifi_ssid', 'your_password')
  ```

- **Robotics**: You built simple robots, like a line follower or a two-wheeled robot, and controlled them using Python.

```
from motor import Motor
motor = Motor(1)  # Create an instance of the motor connected to pin 1
motor.on()  # Start the motor
```

Confidence in Using MicroPython/CircuitPython and Pi

By now, you should have a good understanding of how to use Python for embedded systems. You're ready to tackle more complex projects with confidence!

Here's an example to boost your confidence: controlling a servo motor using PWM.

```
from machine import Pin, PWM
from time import sleep


pwm = PWM(Pin(25))
pwm.freq(50)  # Set frequency to 50Hz


for duty in range(650, 870):  # Change duty cycle from 650 to 870 (1ms to 2ms)
    pwm.duty(duty)
    sleep(0.1)
```

Next Steps: Expanding Your Embedded Python Horizons

Cloud Integration

Integrate your embedded projects with cloud services like AWS IoT, Google Cloud IoT, or Azure IoT Hub.

Example: Publishing sensor data to an MQTT topic using the umqtt library and receiving messages.

```
from umqtt import MQTTClient
import machine
```

```
client = MQTTClient('your_client_id', 'your_broker_ip')
client.connect()
client.publish('sensors/topic', str(machine.ADC(0).read()))
```

Home Automation

Control smart home devices using Python and protocols like MQTT or custom HTTP APIs.

Example: Controlling a smart LED bulb connected to an ESP8266 using MQTT.

```
from umqtt import MQTTClient
import json

def on_connect(mqtt, userdata):
    mqtt.subscribe('home/led')
    mqtt.publish('home/led', json.dumps({'state': 'ON'}))

client = MQTTClient('esp8266', 'your_broker_ip', on_connect)
client.connect()
```

Advanced Robotics

Build more complex robots and explore advanced control algorithms.

Example: Implementing a PID controller for a two-wheeled robot to follow a line using the pymotor library.

```
from pymotor import Motor, LineFollower
import time

motor = Motor(1)
lf = LineFollower(Motor.PIN_LEFT, Motor.PIN_RIGHT)

while True:
```

```
error = lf.error()
correction = pid.calc(error)
motor.set_speed(correction, -correction)
time.sleep(0.05)
```

Further Learning: Advanced Topics

Real-Time Operating Systems (RTOS)

Explore RTOS like FreeRTOS or ChibiOS to manage tasks and resources efficiently in your embedded projects.

Example: Creating a simple task using FreeRTOS in MicroPython.

```python
import _thread
import time


def task():
    while True:
        print('Task running')
        time.sleep(1)


_thread.start_new_thread(task, ())
```

CAN Bus and Other Communication Protocols

Learn about other communication protocols like CAN Bus, I2C, SPI, or RS-485 for more complex projects.

Example: Sending a message over CAN Bus using the canio library.

```python
from canio import CANBus
from time import sleep


bus = CANBus('RX', 'TX')
msg = {'id': 0x123, 'data': bytes([0xAA, 0xBB])}
```

```
while True:
    bus.send(msg)
    sleep(1)
```

Exploring Other Languages and Boards

C/C++ for Drivers and New Python Boards (micro:bit, Pyboard)

Learn C/C++ to write efficient drivers and explore new Python boards like micro:bit or Pyboard.

Example: Blinking an LED using C on a BBC micro:bit.

```c
#include "main.h"

int main() {
    set_led(LED_GREEN, true);
    sleep_ms(500);
    set_led(LED_GREEN, false);
    sleep_ms(500);
}
```

Community Engagement

Join forums and communities like the official MicroPython or CircuitPython forums, Discord servers, or Reddit to learn from others and share your projects.

- MicroPython Forum: https://forum.micropython.org/
- CircuitPython Discord: https://discord.gg/94FHm3
- r/MicroPython on Reddit: https://www.reddit.com/r/MicroPython/

Staying Updated with MicroPython/CircuitPython Releases

Follow the official blogs and newsletters to stay updated about new features, updates, and releases.

- MicroPython Blog: https://micropython.org/blog/
- Adafruit Learning System for CircuitPython: https://learn.adafruit.com/circuitpython

Final Encouragement: Prototype in Python, Iterate Rapidly, Contribute Back

Python allows you to prototype quickly and iterate rapidly. Don't hesitate to contribute back to the community by sharing your projects, writing tutorials, or even contributing code.

Example: Sharing a simple project on the MicroPython Forum.

---
title: My first LED blink project using MicroPython on an ESP8266
author: Your Name

Here's my first MicroPython project blinking an LED connected to GPIO2 on an ESP8266:

```python
from machine import Pin
import utime

led = Pin(2, Pin.OUT)

while True:
    led.on()
    utime.sleep(0.5)
    led.off()
    utime.sleep(0.5)
```